Praise for *Pretreatment Across Multiple Fields of Practice*

Pretreatment Across Multiple Fields of Practice shows Jay Levy's radically humane framework for human relationships is now generating positive change well beyond its starting point: people on the street. This new collection demonstrates that Pretreatment thinking offers people working with all kinds of human services a powerful, practical framework for engagement, for change and ultimately for healing. As a keen follower of Jay's publications, it is exciting to see how people are using his ideas to drive forward so much positive work. Our world can seem quite dark at the moment, this book will give you hope.

Alex Bax, Chief Executive (London)
Pathway – Homeless & Inclusion Health (pathway.org.uk)

The stories shared by the authors are powerful examples of the importance of building therapeutic alliances that are based on the radical notion that the people we are trying to help are the experts in their own lives. Like many of the book's contributors, I wish I had learned of the Pretreatment model earlier in my career as its approach is transformative. This book should be required reading for everyone working in the human services field!

Kiko Malin, MPH, MSW
Public Health Director, Town of Amherst

I found it clever how Levy used Pretreatment values of collaboration and inclusive relationships throughout the book, utilising people's relevant experiences and strengths to promote wellbeing. Each contributing author shows their passion for the work, giving specific examples and providing the reader with feelings of validation, not shying away from honesty and transparency around their views, particularly around the NHS 'medical model.' So many times, I said "yes!" out loud in agreement whilst reading.

Emma Marsh
Clinical Team Manager, LYPFT Rough Sleepers Mental Health Service
Chair of the nationwide Setting up Services Forum for Homelessness

Pre-treatment Therapy is as important a concept in working with people who have experienced so-called 'complex trauma,' or people with the characteristics associated with diagnoses of personality disorders, as mentalisation has become; indeed, it provides the basic groundwork of mentalisation in working with people with complex emotional needs. This book is therefore essential reading for anyone trying to work with, or commission services for, people who have experienced multiple or compound trauma.

As Levy, Connolly, and others argue in this important book, the concept of Pre-treatment Therapy is of major applicability way beyond the field of homelessness: its ideas and concepts should be core reading for psychologists and psychiatrists and indeed anybody hoping to work with people affected by chronic experiences of trauma in a psychologically informed way. It's often said that service providers should 'meet people where they are.' This book explains why and how to do that.

Dr Peter Cockersell, DPsych
Psychoanalytic Psychotherapist
Consultant in Psychologically Informed Environments
Chief Executive of Community Housing and Therapy

Jay's legacy as a leader, mentor, advocate, and practitioner has transformed thousands of lives for the better and I could not be happier to see his light continue to shine in the form of this wonderful collection of work.

Keith Wales, MSW, LICSW
Vice President of Homeless Services
Eliot Community Human Services

A Shintoist saying is, "There are many mountains to God, and many paths up each mountain." This book has chapters describing a variety of approaches that are all based on respect, compassion, decency, patience, and acceptance. Individually, each is powerful. Combined, as this book recommends, they have the potential to transform the world.

Bob Rich, PhD
Healesville, Victoria, Australia
Author of *From Depression to Contentment*

The authors of this book strongly advocate for moving away from medical and siloed models of care where an individual is expected to fit into a medicalized system with a focus on key performance indicators, tick boxes and repeated assessments, which only retraumatise individuals leaving further damage and disengagement. A Pretreatment approach focuses on principles that are person centred, holistic, and with a model that is strength-and-asset based with systems being solution focused and integrated. Through this psychosocial model of engagement, there is also a move away from discrimination, stigma, and blame to a model that is integrated and inclusive.

Jane Cook
Queen's Nurse, Registered General Nurse, Health Visitor
Complex Needs Manager, Groundswell

With Jay Levy as a colleague, supervisor, manager, and friend, and with street outreach workers as a team, for years I had the benefit of learning "Pretreatment" by example, conversation, and processing. We seldom used the term, but we consistently learned "it."

When I moved from street outreach to treatment and support services to houseless people who have a sexual offending history, Pretreatment followed. As demonstrated throughout the varied narratives in Jay's latest book, the new environment brought different circumstances, different stories, and different systems... but the core of our work followed, with the Pretreatment foundational words of my mentor that "I would be called to approach my work with great humility and that I would not be owning the process, nor dictating the terms of our interactions."

I would not have grown doing the work any other way and I was touched by the results.

Richard Hendrick, MSW, LICSW (unfolding, not retired)
Author of *Not for Nuttin':*
A journey with some folks without homes and me.

Pretreatment Across Multiple Fields of Practice

Trauma Informed Approach to Homelessness and Beyond

Edited by Jay S. Levy, MSW
with Louise Levy, MEd

Loving Healing Press

Ann Arbor, MI

Pretreatment Across Multiple Fields of Practice: Trauma Informed Approach to Homelessness and Beyond
Edited by Jay S. Levy, MSW with Louise Levy, MEd

ISBN 978-1-61599-857-9 Paperback
ISBN 978-1-61599-858-6 Hardcover
ISBN 978-1-61599-859-3 eBook

Loving Healing Press
5145 Pontiac Trail
Ann Arbor, MI 48105
Toll free: 888-761-6268 (USA/CAN) FAX: 734-663-6861
info@LHPress.com
www.LHPress.com

Distributed by Ingram Book Group (USA, Canada, EU, UK)

Library of Congress Cataloging-in-Publication Data

Names: Levy, Jay S., 1961- editor.

Title: Pretreatment across multiple fields of practice : trauma informed approach to homelessness and beyond / edited by Jay S. Levy, MSW ; with Louise Levy, MEd.

Description: Ann Arbor, MI : Loving Healing Press, 2025. | Includes bibliographical references and index. | Summary: "Outlines working principles that guide practitioners in the art of building authentic and effective working partnerships with people experiencing homelessness and other traumas, while minimizing re-traumatization and creating psychological safety. Areas of concentration cover the gamut of Pretreatment principles including street medicine, homeless outreach, supportive housing, pre-treatment therapy, and other disciplines"-- Provided by publisher.

Identifiers: LCCN 2024048602 (print) | LCCN 2024048603 (ebook) | ISBN 9781615998579 (paperback) | ISBN 9781615998586 (hardcover) | ISBN 9781615998593 (epub)

Subjects: LCSH: Homeless persons--Services for--United States. | Homeless persons--Services for--Great Britain. | Homeless persons--Mental health services--United States. | Homeless persons--Mental health services--Great Britain. | Homelessness--United States. | Homelessness--Great Britain.

Classification: LCC HV4505 .P745 2025 (print) | LCC HV4505 (ebook) | DDC 362.5/920973--dc23/eng/20250123

LC record available at https://lccn.loc.gov/2024048602

LC ebook record available at https://lccn.loc.gov/2024048603

Contents

Table of Figures

Dedication

To all those without homes, and those who have survived homelessness, and to the Outreach workers, Nurses, Doctors, Case Managers, Experts from Experience, and others who help the most vulnerable among us. May their courage, strength and dedication serve as an inspiration to achieve better health and greater equity for all.

Proceeds from this Book

The author has pledged 25% of book royalties and other related book profits to a 501c(3) charity that supports the cause of significantly reducing and/or ending homelessness.

About Client Confidentiality

The case illustrations depicted in this book are based on actual persons and events from our field experiences. However, names, places and events have been altered as warranted to protect client confidentiality.

US Foreword

Jay and Louise Levy continue to expand and deepen the impact of Pretreatment through their latest publication, *Pretreatment Across Multiple Fields of Practice: Trauma Informed Approach to Homelessness and Beyond* (edited by Jay S. Levy, MSW with Louise Levy, MEd). Based on Jay's many decades of clinical experience and supported by an impressive body of evidence-based references, the Pretreatment framework is proving to be a powerful tool for understanding the principles of inclusion, solidarity and the healing community. Those of us who have been working with people stuck under "the iceberg of pre-contemplative change" are deeply grateful to Jay for clarifying the principles of our work. My more than three decades of street medicine experience validate the wisdom of Jay's Pretreatment model.

Jay and Louise have assembled an impressive panel of experts who care for excluded and traumatized populations. Each discuss their particular field of practice and reveal how the Pretreatment framework has informed their care. By utilizing such a diverse array of contexts, the unifying principles of Pretreatment become even more clear to the reader. Each author brings life to the Pretreatment way of seeing relationships and validates the wisdom of Jay's model from different frames of reference. The sum is greater than the parts, in that one is left feeling inspired that a core set of values can transcend such diverse fields. Those values have been discovered by many of us through decades of intense commitment to the reality of our excluded sisters and brothers, but Pretreatment pulls the threads of those values into a tighter fabric.

Personally, although I am impressed and grateful to Jay for his functional, evidence-based model of care, I am most impressed with his consistent focus on honoring the reality of those who have been excluded. We are long overdue to invert the power dynamic of systems-centered "care industries." This is a revolutionary perspective many of us have been fighting for. His accessible writing style brings us to the place where we can embrace the challenge of letting go of our agendas and allow those we serve to truly be the authors of their own narratives. This, of course, echoes the work of Paulo Freire and others who have fought to decolonialize the structures that continue to oppress and hold people down. As a representative of the Street Medicine Institute, and more importantly, the global street medicine movement, Jay's work is a beacon not just to light the path we are on, but to guide us towards a better place.

Jim Withers, MD
Medical Director and Founder of Pittsburgh Mercy's Operation Safety Net
Medical Director and Founder of the Street Medicine Institute
Assistant Clinical Professor of Medicine, University of Pittsburgh

UK Foreword

Working in mental health services in the NHS can be difficult. Services are over-stretched, and staff are under pressure to diagnose, assess risk, and arrive at a management plan as efficiently as possible. But as this book shows, there is another way of doing things.

When I first started work in a mental health team for people sleeping rough, it was a marked jump in culture. I was only three years into psychiatric training, but I had already started to accept the routines: invite people into clinic, fire a bunch of questions at them, and if they don't turn up three times, discharge them to the GP. I had just passed my membership exams and felt secure in the knowledge that I knew all the subheadings for the thorough psychiatric history that was so prized by assessors.

It soon became clear that this approach wasn't going to work at all in my new job. There was no point in sitting in a clinic if no one came in, and no point having a list of questions to ask if no-one stuck around to answer them. The team I had joined was doing something different: going out looking for people, finding ways to get to know them, and then forming a connection, and working out together what help was needed and how to provide it. It was a change of perspective that I loved from the outset, but for a young doctor it was daunting: what to say? How to find common ground with people whose lives were so different from my own?

Luckily, the team I was part of (the Focus team in North London) was full of immensely dedicated, experienced and talented professionals—social workers, nurses, psychologists, and occupational therapists. I owe a huge debt of gratitude to them for all they taught me on our joint outreach shifts. By watching, listening, and through a certain amount of trial and error, I grew in confidence and learnt what felt like a very different way to practice psychiatry. Most of all, of course, I have learnt from my patients: in that job, in my subsequent posts in addictions psychiatry, and indeed in my clinical practice now, they make it abundantly clear whether or not I am getting things right.

Almost twenty years on, as a consultant psychiatrist in another mental health team for rough sleepers on the other side of the Thames, I see new staff members going through the same challenges. Some are quicker to adapt than others—it must be said that the change of pace often seems particularly difficult for doctors, steeped as we are in the medical model. They are often shocked that we don't fire a battery of questions at new people we meet, as described so eloquently by Matthew S. Bennett in chapter 2. Such questions may indeed be re-traumatising for the patient, but which are perhaps a comfort blanket for practitioners who are wary of criticism that they've missed something out.

I was a latecomer to Jay Levy's work in Pretreatment and Pretreatment Therapy, first hearing about it at Pathways Homeless and Inclusion Health conference in 2021. But when I heard Jay speak it was with a great wave of recognition—this was what I had been trying to do for all those years. I subsequently read one of his previous books, *Pretreatment In Action*, and wished that I had been able to read it back in 2006. It would have saved me a lot of heartache and spared my patients a lot of painful consultations. Now I press that book into the hands of new starters in my team: it is a perfect introduction to our work and means I no longer need my incoherent explanations along the lines of "you just need to get people talking." Many I think are buoyed in confidence by the idea that it is an approach and therapy that has a name and is written out—something that can be learned, rather than intuited. Permission for working in a more flexible style is granted.

I have often thought that Pretreatment is applicable far beyond the world of outreach to people who are sleeping rough. In their new book, Jay and Louise draw together a collection of essays from other settings in which it has been successful: in the UK and the US, from homeless hostel and supportive-housing[1] settings to the school room—it is heartening and inspiring to read. I hope that it is widely read, not just in the homeless world but far beyond. I suspect that there are many more settings

[1] Supportive housing settings range from 24/7 staffed Safe Haven programs to affordable scattered site housing with ongoing case management services.

where a Pretreatment approach can be used, and that in fact every practitioner working within mental health can learn from it. All of us meet those who are vulnerable, who are reluctant to ask for help. How much more rewarding it is to be curious, to try to build a relationship, rather than closing the door!

I hope too that *Pretreatment Across Multiple Fields of Practice* is read by those who plan and commission mental health services. The lessons learnt by Chris Brown and Dan Southall in setting up their new team in Hull, which they describe in chapter 7, are valuable ones that can be used wherever new services are being devised. Overall from this book, there is a strong message that if people are "hard to engage," then those who are doing the engaging are going about it the wrong way. Food for thought for those with the power to change things.

Finally, it has to be said that making use of Pretreatment does not only benefit the recipient, but also those who practice it. Perhaps, working in human services does not have to be so difficult. Many authors in this book talk about the model saving them from burnout, and I can relate to that. Early in my career I started to have the jaded feeling that assessments were done for the benefit of the service, not the patient, which did not square with what I had been taught, that the assessment *should be* a therapeutic tool in itself. It is surely that sort of dissonance that leads to burnout and I feel fortunate and privileged to have quickly got away from it. I would suggest that Pretreatment gives us permission to go back to the basic idea of trying to help people (surely the reason we all went into the job!) and allows us to find the joy in our clinical work.

As Jay says, we are all human, and at its heart Pretreatment in any setting is about making connections as one human being to another. What can be more satisfying, more life-enhancing, than that?

Dr Jenny Drife
Consultant Psychiatrist, START team for People Sleeping Rough
South London and Maudsley NHS Foundation Trust
Advisor to the Royal College of Psychiatrists on homelessness and mental health

Preface

The Pursuit of Meaningful Connections and Dialogue

Jay S. Levy

My writing initially served the purpose of getting perspective on the challenging work of outreach to folks who were sleeping rough with complex and multiple needs inclusive of housing, financial hardship, and an array of medical, mental health and addiction concerns. My background in philosophy, psychology and social work helped me to integrate practice and theory into a model to guide our mission. At the start of the new millennium (2000), I published a journal article introducing this approach to others and formally coined it "Pretreatment." Over the past two decades, its word and practice has spread throughout the US and UK.

Honestly, it is a bit surprising to hear the declarations from other professionals on how a Pretreatment perspective really spoke to them and positively changed their approach to helping. Yet, I have heard this repeatedly.

Their ongoing requests for new presentations, training and writing has brought us here!

What is different about this project is that applications of Pretreatment across multiple systems of care have matured. This sets the stage for practitioners and others to tell their stories directly from the field, part and parcel of the challenges and successes of their various human service programs, staff, and the people they serve. There is much to share here, while the pursuit of meaningful connections and dialogue continues in our workplaces and beyond.

This time around, I will put on my editor's hat, with some significant assistance from my life partner, Louise Levy, award-winning environmental and agricultural studies HS teacher, and my favorite grammatologist. The steps taken on a thousand walks with Louise provide just the right shift in perspective. Our conversations shine a light on the true value of a Pretreatment perspective and how to communicate that value to others.

I am eternally grateful to all those from both the US and UK who have contributed chapters and have done the hard work of integrating Pretreatment into their field of practice. Their contributions range from Outreach Counseling and Case Management, to Trauma based Therapy and Special Education, as well as development of programs and greater systems of care.

The healing power of person-centered relationships is at the heart of a Pretreatment philosophy and the narratives throughout this text highlight the indisputable importance of meaningful connections and dialogue for all of us. As I am fond of saying "We are Human… All too Human,"[2] so what is helpful with those we serve applies equally to our staff and to our own lives. We invite you to see yourself and your work in the stories contained in this volume.

[2] I first came across this quote through the writings of Friedrich Nietzsche. In fact, he even published a book entitled, *Human, All too Human* (1878).

1 Introducing Pretreatment: Outreach Counseling for People with Significant Trauma & Loss

Jay S. Levy

> If we could look into each other's hearts and understand the unique challenges each of us faces, I think we would treat each other much more gently, with more love, patience, tolerance, and care.
>
> Marvin J. Ashton (1992)

Far too many people are desperately in need and yet are afraid to hope. The most vulnerable among us are often not actively seeking help and may even be pre-contemplative[3] of their own complex-multiple needs. This is an understandable and protective stance to a significant history of trauma and loss that is often compounded by negative experiences with human service workers and systems of care (toxic help[4]). Some have experienced so many unkept promises or perceived personal failures in addition to the loss of critical supportive relationships that they reside in a perpetual state of learned helplessness.

---

[3] Pre-contemplation is the first stage of Prochaska's and DiClemente's Change Model. It denotes a lack of awareness or concern about a particular problem or its severity and therefore not considering or contemplating options for help or healing. If our interventions are successfully aligned with this stage, it may help the person to enter the second Change Model stage of Contemplation and eventually taking action toward positive change.

[4] John Conolly coined the phrase, "toxic help'" and discusses this in Chapter 8. It is when people reach out for assistance and the "help" they purportedly receive makes things worse.

Since the late 1980s, I found this to be common among people who had experienced long-term homelessness. On a basic level we were failing to reach out to those who were most in need. There was a clear calling for a more effective and impactful outreach counseling practice that could not only facilitate access to affordable housing, but also recovery options to address the vestiges of significant trauma and loss.

I first pioneered "Pretreatment" as an approach to help people without homes who presented with complex trauma issues in an article published by the *Families in Society* journal, entitled "Homeless Outreach: On the Road to Pretreatment Alternatives" (Levy, 2000). This was the outgrowth of my witnessing too many people being ignored by a treatment-biased culture. People who were continually refused services because they were not raising their hands and actively requesting help for healthcare inclusive of mental health and/or addiction issues. In response to this dilemma, a Pretreatment philosophy was developed from an outreach perspective.

Over the past several years, applications of Pretreatment have spread, aiding a variety of programs and staff to reach those who were often deemed "too high risk," "non-compliant," "beyond service capabilities," "ineligible," or "not ready" to partake in services. The fields of practice have ranged from outreach, street medicine, and housing support to clinical services that address trauma, as well as education to better serve those with complex multiple needs.

What is it about Pretreatment that allows for such great flexibility across multiple fields of practice? The answer is rooted in its four basic tenets of care (Levy, 2013):

- The initial task is to literally and figuratively get where the person is at.
- Our interventions are informed by how our words and actions resonate in the person's world.
- We foster a trusting relationship that upholds client autonomy as the foundation of our work, while utilizing common language construction as our main tool for facilitating productive dialogue.
- We instill a sense of hope and possibility for positive change.

I think that one can see from the outset how these basic tenets have universal appeal for human services, as most if not all human services can be relationship-driven. In fact, a Pretreatment model is primarily based on the research that has demonstrated the importance of person-centered and goal-focused work.

What is Pretreatment?

The term "Pretreatment" (Levy, 2000, pp. 360-368; Levy, 2010, pp. 13-16) initially appeared as "Pretreatment Variables" through research that predicted successful outcomes for addiction and recovery treatment approaches (Joe et al., 1998, p. 1177; Miller & Rollnick 1991, pp. 5-29; Salloum et al., 1998, p.35). Psychologist and researcher Bruce Wampold (2001) took this a step further by conducting a meta-analysis of pretreatment variables on the success of different counseling methods for addressing mental illness. He concluded that therapeutic models mattered less as a predictor for success than an array of general factors such as the client's hope and expectation for change, belief in the effectiveness of the therapy, and a positive working alliance between the client and therapist.

The main conclusions from research on both mental illness and addictions support the value of client-centered approaches (Rogers, 1957; Levy, 1998; Wampold, 2001), the importance of motivation and problem recognition, as well as the belief in the therapeutic model or approach by both counselor and client. Other studies on assisting people with severe mental illness uphold the effectiveness of psychosocial rehabilitation principles (Anthony et al., 1990), which instill hope and motivation by being goal-focused, rather than problem-centered. An integral part of the work is for counselor and client to jointly identify barriers to achieving one's objectives and thereby develop strategies to overcome these obstacles. This is a goal-centered approach that helps people to recognize certain concerns over time based on their aspirations, rather than being dependent upon a person presenting with initial problems and/or declaring themselves in need of help.

Most people who experience the detrimental effects of homelessness and trauma are struggling just to survive and meet their immediate needs of health and safety. The research literature on people who experience homelessness (Babidge, Buhrich, & Butler, 2001; Burt et al. 1999, p. xix;

Hwang, 2000; Johnson & Haigh (Eds), 2012; McMillan et al. 2015; O'Connell, 2005) confirms the high risk of premature death and increased rates of chronic health issues such as arthritis, diabetes, and cancer, as well as significant rates of psychological trauma and traumatic brain injury (TBI).

The conclusions from this type of research, coupled with the persistence of a treatment-biased culture that does not adequately provide access for people without homes who have significant healthcare concerns, indicate the need for a Pretreatment approach. It is relationship-driven work based on five guiding principles of care (Levy, 2000) as follows:

- Relationship Formation—Promote trust and respect client autonomy via Stages of Engagement resulting in a client-centered relationship that is goal-driven.
- Common Language Construction—Listen, understand and utilize a person's words, ideas and values in an effort to develop effective communication.
- Ecological Considerations—Support the process of Transition and Adaptation to new ideas, people, environments, housing, and recovery, etc.
- Facilitate Change—Utilize Stages of Change Model and Motivational Interviewing techniques to facilitate positive change.
- Promote Safety—Apply Crisis Intervention and Harm Reduction Strategies to reduce risk, increase safety, promote stability, and embrace the opportunity for positive change.

Pretreatment (Levy, 2010) is defined as:

> ...an approach that enhances safety while promoting transition to housing (e.g., housing first options), and/or treatment and recovery alternatives through client-centered supportive interventions that develop goals and motivation to create positive change.

An outreach counseling process based on a Pretreatment philosophy affords us the opportunity to become both interpreters and bridge builders (Levy, 2013). Potential resources and services are therefore reinterpreted and reframed so the client can more fully consider these options and their potential impacts. This is the first major step toward building a bridge to needed resources and services that include housing, education, vocational training, treatment, and recovery options. It is a bridge consisting of a safe and trusting relationship between worker and client, as well as a common language that fosters communication. This aligns with our striving to understand people's values and stories in a manner that dignifies the meaning or purpose of their narratives. Our mission is to reach out and engage vulnerable people in an open dialogue that leads to improved access to healthcare and a stable place to live promoting meaningful connections with others and a better quality of life.

A fuller conception of outreach counseling is derived from a Pretreatment approach that includes its ten guidelines (See Table 1-1 on p. 7) and the stages of Engagement (Levy, 2011; Levy, 2013) as represented here (See Table 1-2 on p. 8), based upon my integration of Eric Erikson's (1968) Psychosocial Developmental stages and Germain & Gitterman's (1980) Ecological phases. This includes developmental-stage-sensitive strategies and interventions to help guide the worker throughout the outreach counseling process.

Pretreatment and its related texts and training have been utilized by human services organizations throughout Massachusetts, New York, Texas, and California, among other states, via Street Medicine and Health Care for the Homeless practitioners, shelter case managers, After Incarceration service providers, Experts by Lived Experience (Peer Network), Homeless Outreach teams, and Housing First staff. It is part of several recommended reading lists and course syllabi at universities throughout the States.

Pretreatment has been adapted to provide guidance to homelessness services by UK charities (e.g., The Connection St. Martins in the Fields Homeless Day Centre and Outreach Team, Trafalgar Square, London) and Pre-treatment Therapy at the CLCH NHS Trust Westminster Homeless Health Counseling Service in Soho, London. It is endorsed by the Faculty for Homeless and Inclusion Health, and it is an intervention model recommended by several British NHS mental health/psychological services commissioners (e.g., Hull, Leeds) for serving people sleeping rough who have complex and multiple needs. Further, a mental health service for people who experience homelessness, explicitly informed by Pretreatment, has just been established in Dublin, Ireland.

A Pretreatment model based on five universal principles of care provides a needed compass for the complexity of our work. It provides a scaffolding for staff to achieve their mission with a greater sense of purpose. It can help vulnerable people to get "unstuck" through person-centered therapeutic relationships that promote open dialogue leading to meaningful individualized goals. This is the key to melting the pre-contemplative iceberg.[5]

This book features several authors who have implemented a Pretreatment approach and have witnessed its positive impact across a variety of settings with people who present with complex trauma and significant challenges. Pretreatment is both a general and flexible guide that promotes quality person-centered care without limiting the creativity of workers and clients.

Together, we can take on the challenge of care to reach out and better serve vulnerable populations in a more equitable and inclusive manner. This means putting aside "readiness" criteria and instead challenging ourselves to be ready to meet people where they are at and foster critical helping relationships and meaningful dialogue that crosses cultural divides. Pretreatment provides us with a guide and the tools to successfully respond to this challenge by providing greater access to a broad spectrum of outreach, education, and healthcare services. I hope that the stories shared, coupled with a demonstrated range of applications, will help inform and guide those who are considering the benefits and challenges of integrating a Pretreatment approach into their own practice and programs.

---

[5] I came across the term "pre-contemplative iceberg" through my correspondence with Dr Jim Withers from the Street medicine Institute.

Table 1-1: 10 Guidelines for Outreach Counseling (Pretreatment Perspective)

1. Meet clients (both literally and figuratively) where they are at!
2. The relationship is most important — Promote trust and respect autonomy.
3. Develop a common language of shared words, ideas and values.
4. Be goal centered — Join the person in setting goals that resonate well in his or her world.
5. Mutually define or characterize particular difficulties to achieving goals and jointly develop strategies or plans.
6. Carefully support transitions to new ideas, relationships (stages of engagement), environments, resources, and treatment (bridge client language to treatment language).
7. Promote Safety via Harm Reduction strategies and Crisis Intervention techniques.
8. Utilize crisis as an opportunity to promote positive change.
9. Respect the process of change—understand its stages and relevant interventions.
10. Understand the person's narrative and integrate a person's sense of meaning or purpose with movement toward positive change.

Originally published: Levy, J. S. (2011). *Homeless Outreach & Housing First: Lessons Learned*

Table 1-2: Outreach-Counseling Developmental Model

Ecological Phase	Psychosocial Challenge	Strategies & Interventions
Pre-Engagement Initial Phase	Trust vs. Mistrust Issues of Safety	Observation, Identify Potential Client, Respect Personal Space, Safety Assessment, Attempt Verbal and Nonverbal Communication, Offer Essential Need Items, Listen for Client's Language, Establish Initial Communication, etc.
Engagement Initial Phase	Trust vs. Mistrust Issues of Dependency Boundary Issues	Communicate with Empathy and Authenticity, Learn Client's Language, Active Listening by Reflecting Client's Words, ideas, and Values, Identify and Reinforce Client Strengths, Provide Unconditional Regard, Avoid Power Struggles, Emphasis on Joining the Resistance, Introduction of Roles, Begin and Continue Development of Healthy Boundaries, Establish Ongoing Communication, Identify Current Life Stressors, etc.
Contracting Initial Phase	Autonomy vs. Shame Issues of Control Initiative vs. Guilt	Further Define Roles and Boundaries, Address Shame by Universalizing Human Frailty and Reviewing Client Strengths, Point Out Discrepancy and Explore Ambivalence, Negotiate Reachable Goals to Alleviate Life Stressors, Explore Client History in Relation to Goals, Determine Eligibility for Potential Resources and Services Regarding Client Interests, Further Define Shared Objectives by Utilizing Client Language, Jointly Consider Housing Options, etc.
Contract Implementation Ongoing Work Phase	Initiative vs. Guilt Issues of Stability Industry vs. Inferiority	Joint Assessment of Goals, Strengths, and Obstacles, Identify and Address Fear, Shame, Guilt, and Anger Issues Through Listening, Joining, Validating and Redirect Focus to Achievable Tasks, Review and Reinforce Current Coping Strategies, Promote Self care, Education re: Symptom Management, Further Develop Skills and Supports, Refer to Indicated Services, Enhance Coping Strategies, Mobilize Client Strengths, Support Transition and Adaptation to New Programs, Services and Housing, Reinforce Positive Change.
Termination Ending Phase	Relationship Identity vs. Confusion of Roles Boundary Issues Issues of Loss	Review the Work Completed Together, Emphasize Gains, Share Feelings of Loss, Connect to Past losses, Differentiate, and Explore as Needed, Reinforce and Consolidate Change, Review and Reinforce Support Systems, Review and Redefine Provider Roles, as well as Client-Worker Relationship, Redirect to Established Support Systems

* Many of the interventions listed are applicable to different phases (stages) of the outreach-counseling process, yet have particular relevance to the indicated stage.

References

Anthony, W., Cohen, M., & Farkas, M. (1990). *Psychiatric rehabilitation.* Boston University:Center For Psychiatric Rehabilitation.

Ashton, M.J. (1992) "The Tongue Can Be a Sharp Sword," *Ensign*, May 1992, 20. https://www.churchofjesuschrist.org/study/ensign/1992/05/the-tongue-can-be-a-sharp-sword?lang=eng

Berger, P., and Luckman, T. (1966). *The social construction of reality.* New York: Doubleday.

Babidge, N.C., Buhrich, N., & Butler, T. (2001, Feb.). Mortality among homeless people with schizophrenia in Sydney, Australia: 10-year follow-up. *Acta Psychiatrica Scandinavica*, (103)2, 105-110.

Burt, M.R.and Aron, L.Y. (2000). *America's homeless II: Populations and services.* Washington, DC: The Urban Institute.

Burt, M.R., Aron, L.Y., Douglas, T., Valente, J., Lee, E., Iwen, B. (1999, August). Homelessness: Programs and the people they serve. Findings of a national survey of homeless assistance: 1996 summary report. Washington, DC: The Urban Institute.

Erikson, E.H. (1968). *Identity: youth and crisis.* New York: Norton.

Germain, C.B., & Gitterman, A. (1980). *The life model of social work process.* New York: Columbia University Press.

Hopper, E., Bassuk, E., & Olivet, J., (2010). Shelter from the Storm: Trauma-Informed Care in Homelessness Services Settings. *The Open Health Services & Policy Journal.* 3. 80-100.

Hwang, S.W., Lebow, J.J., Bierer, M.F., O'Connell, J., Orav, E.J., & Brennan,T.A. (1998). Risk factors for deaths in homeless adults in Boston. *Archives of Internal Medicine*, 158(13): 1454-1460.

Hwang, S.W. (2000). Mortality among men using homeless shelters in Toronto, Ontario. *Journal of the American Medical Association*, 283(16): 2152-2157.

Joe, G.W., Simpson, D.D., & Broome, K.M. (1998). Effects of readiness for drug abuse treatment on client retention and assessment of process. *Addiction*, 93(8), 1177-1190.

Johnson R & Haigh R, Editors. (2012) *Complex Trauma and its effects; perspectives on creating an environment for recovery* (Brighton: Pavilion)

Levy, J.S. (1998, Fall). Homeless outreach: A developmental model. *Psychiatric Rehabilitation Journal*, 22(2), 123-131.

Levy, J.S. (2000, July-Aug.). Homeless outreach: On the road to pretreatment alternatives. *Families in Society: The Journal of Contemporary Human Services*, 81(4), 360-368.

Levy, J.S. (2010). *Homeless narratives and pretreatment pathways: From words to housing*. Ann Arbor, MI: Loving Healing Press.

Levy, J.S. (2011). *Homeless outreach and housing first: Lessons learned*. Ann Arbor, MI: Loving Healing Press.

Levy, J.S. (2013). *Pretreatment guide for homeless outreach and housing first: Helping couples, youth, and unaccompanied adults*. Ann Arbor, MI: Loving Healing Press.

McMillan, T.M., Laurie, M., Oddy, M., Menzies, M., Stewart, E., & Wainman-Lefley, J. (2015). Head injury and mortality in the homeless. *Journal of Neurotrauma. 32(2)*: 116-119

Miller, W.R. & Rollnick, S. (1991). *Motivational interviewing: Preparing people to change addictive behavior*. New York: Guilford.

O'Connell, J.J. *Premature Mortality in Homeless Populations: A Review of the Literature,* 19 pages. Nashville: National Health Care for the Homeless Council, Inc., 2005.

O'Connell, J.J, Swain S. Rough sleepers: A five-year prospective study in Boston, 1999-2003. Presentation, Tenth Annual Ending Homelessness Conference, Massachusetts Housing and Shelter Alliance, Waltham, MA 2005.

Prochaska, J.O. & DiClemente, C.C. (1982). Trans theoretical therapy: Toward a more integrative model of change. *Psychotherapy: Theory, Research, and Practice*. 19, 276-288.

Rogers, C.R. (1957). The necessary and sufficient conditions for therapeutic personality change. Journal of Consulting Psychology, 21, 95-103.

Salloum, I.M., Moss, H.B., Daley, D.C., & Cornelius, J.R. (1998). Drug use problem awareness and treatment readiness in dual diagnosis patients. *American Journal on Addictions*, 7(1).

Wampold, B.E. (2001) *The great psychotherapy Debate: Models, methods, findings*. Mahwah, New Jersey: Lawrence Erlbaum Associates.

2 Pretreatment: Connecting Paradigms

Matthew S. Bennett

> A paradigm shift is an important change that happens when the usual way of thinking about or doing something is replaced by a new and different way.
>
> Merriam-Webster (2023)

We live in a golden age. As a student of the history of psychology, I cannot point to another period where the science of the human mind evolved as rapidly. In my thirty-year career, I had the privilege of participating in these paradigm shifts that transformed the field of housing, HIV, criminal justice, education, health care, and psychology in which I work.

After I completed my graduate program in psychology in 2000, neurobiology and trauma-informed care, along with supporting research in attachment, epigenetics, and mindfulness, I was immediately struck by the difficulties of applying this learning to real-life situations in the field. While science challenges us to evolve our understanding and approaches to helping others, the complexity of these areas requires years of study to fully understand, much less integrate that understanding into our work of helping others.

The human mind needs models to tackle complexity. In my book, *Connecting Paradigms* (Bennett, 2017), I sought to position the evolving science in a way that supports practical approaches to helping people make complex behavioral changes. I worked to create a simple model incorporating the paradigm-shifting power of trauma-informed care,

Motivational Interviewing, neurobiology, stages of change, harm reduction, and mindfulness that people could implement as soon as they read the final chapter.

Then I met Jay Levy and learned about his efforts to establish a Pretreatment approach as a guiding philosophy for helping others. I still remember my first thought, where was this guy and his model in 2015 and 2016 when I wrote *Connecting Paradigms* and its supplement *Talking about Trauma & Change* (Bennett, 2018)? Unfortunately, I was unaware of his work. Not only does Pretreatment align with the science and philosophy of *Connecting Paradigms,* it also provides a model to address the most critical stage of any healing or change journey: how we build trust and relationships with people early in their change journey.

As I start conceptualizing the tenth Anniversary edition of *Connecting Paradigms*, Pretreatment will play a prominent role. When you publish a book, it locks in your thinking on the printed page. While my introduction to Jay and Pretreatment came after my book was written, Jay's work has found a prominent place in my thinking and trainings since meeting him, interviewing him on my podcasts, and reading his books.

In this chapter, I am excited to preview my thinking about the role of Pretreatment in our rapidly evolving understanding of human behavior. I am honored to contribute to the development of Pretreatment. I believe this helps expose even more people to Jay's thinking and the importance of Pretreatment in delivering Trauma-Informed Care, Harm Reduction, and Motivational Interviewing. Pretreatment provides the umbrella for integrating these perspectives into an accessible guide for human service workers to assist vulnerable people with multiple-complex needs across a variety of settings.

Trauma-Informed Care

According to the Substance Abuse and Mental Health Services Administration or SAMHSA (2014):

> A program, organization, or system that is trauma-informed realizes the widespread impact of trauma and understands potential paths for recovery; recognizes the signs and symptoms of trauma in people, families, staff, and others involved with the system; and responds by fully integrating knowledge about

trauma into policies, procedures, and practices, and seeks to actively resist re-traumatization.

Since writing *Connecting Paradigms*, the collective knowledge about the impact of trauma has rapidly expanded throughout our culture. While I could list the things I do not love about getting older, one of the things I value is perspective. When I first learned about the Adverse Childhood Experience Study (Felitti et al.,1998) in 2003, it was hard to find enough people interested in the topic to fill a breakfast table for a monthly meeting I organized in Denver, Colorado.

Over a decade later, I thought the movement had progressed and the world might need a book on a trauma-informed approach to Motivational Interviewing. Almost a decade after starting to write *Connecting Paradigms*, trauma knowledge informs thinking throughout our society. I often muse, "When Oprah Winfrey writes a book about your passion, things change!"

Those who dedicated their careers to the trauma-informed care movement can marvel at the progress. At the same time, we realize that the challenge is not over. Now that the world knows about trauma, how do we use that knowledge to transform our approaches and systems? Pretreatment provides a crucial approach to inform our work in this next stage of the paradigm shift.

A primary focus of any trauma-informed approach is on preventing re-traumatization. Re-traumatization occurs when something about the current environment triggers memories of past trauma. When first working with people with trauma histories, we have no idea what triggers might evoke a re-traumatization response. Pretreatment provides a beautiful and straightforward way to minimize re-traumatization, especially early in the helping relationship (Levy, 2000; Bloom & Farragher, 2011).

If your goal is to re-traumatize people, let me help you do it. In the first contact with a person, before establishing trust and psychological safety, ask them intrusive questions about their past. So many intake assessments include questions such as:

- Are you experiencing domestic or intimate partner violence?
- Do you have any addictions? To what?

- What drugs do you abuse, how much do you take, and how often?
- How many sexual partners have you had in the last year and what type of sex have you had?
- Are you homeless?
- Do you have any diagnosis of mental illness? Have you ever been hospitalized for mental illness?
- Are you unemployed?
- Have you ever been arrested? Are you currently involved in the court system?

I hope most people picking up a book on Pretreatment cringe at these questions. However, each comes from a real-life intake I reviewed over the years in housing, HIV, healthcare, and social service programs. Even if these questions do not trigger re-traumatization, they evoke a sense of shame and unworthiness that haunts most people after a traumatic event. What logic could justify making people relive their most painful and shameful moments?

Even though we might be uncomfortable asking these types of questions, many professionals still have a dilemma. We need to get crucial information to help the individual while not re-traumatizing them in the information-gathering process. Adding to this dilemma, many systems of care require that these re-traumatizing questions continue to get asked on the *first interaction*.

How we traditionally conduct intake interviews fall outside any definition of trauma-informed care. We must stop this process, and I am not alone in advocating loudly to change these harmful practices. However, it does little good to give people insight into the harmful nature of their practices without providing replacement approaches.

Pretreatment answers the question: "How do we make our intake process trauma informed and improve outcomes?" As a trainer and quality improvement consultant, I use Pretreatment Guidelines (Levy, 2013, p. 37) and Jay's books to help organizations and systems revise and improve their intake processes. Pretreatment shifts the focus of the initial contacts from information gathering to relationship building and creating psychological safety. Pretreatment's five principles of care (Levy,

2000; Levy, 2010, p. 130) are relationship formation, common language construction, ecological considerations, promoting safety, and facilitating change. Pretreatment principles of care provide the roadmap to guide these improvement processes. Or as Jay (Levy, 2013, p. 59) states:

> ... it is important that we understand the worlds that our clients construct via their words and ideas, and also grasp what they find to be meaningful. Once we have a better understanding of what people value, we can speak directly to that sensibility and thereby form a trusting relationship based on a common language. Then, future choices and actions can be actively considered. This is the springboard of potentiality!"

I pay attention to the importance of information gathering to ensure that we connect people with the resources and support they need to improve their health and lives. Avoiding re-traumatization and establishing trust and safety creates a relationship where this information comes naturally during empathetic Pretreatment conversations. The people we serve are much more than their struggles and past traumas, and our initial interactions should focus on the person and not just the worst moments of their lives.

If you were to ask me to define trauma-informed care in three words, I would give you: relationships, relationships, relationships! Then I would throw a Judith Herman (1997) quote at you:

> Recovery can take place only within the context of relationships; it cannot occur in isolation. In her renewed connections with other people, the survivor recreates the psychological faculties that were damaged or deformed by the traumatic experience.

As trust builds, the person can better maintain emotional regulation while contemplating difficult behavioral changes. Co-regulation describes the feelings of contentment, calm, and safety that result from talking with someone we trust will treat us with respect and dignity. These feelings of trust build a secure base, allowing for introspection and consideration about the harmful consequences of current thinking and behavior. Levy's (2013, p. 37) *Ten Guidelines for Outreach Counseling* provides both those doing outreach and, I argue, any helping service to build trust in a trauma-informed approach.

Without co-regulation and trust, there is no safety; without safety, there is almost no chance for change and healing. For many people, safety is elusive, as the dangers of intimate partner violence, addiction, homelessness, and lack of basic needs steal their ability to enjoy any security in their lives. Without safety, the person will exist in survival mode. Safety, in this context, is defined as freedom from hurt, injury, or loss. You should consider two types of safety when helping someone make a difficult change or heal from past trauma. The first is physical safety.

Future thinking, goal setting, and emotional regulation are only possible with physical safety and security. If a person must focus on food or shelter, this will dominate their attention. Similarly, an adult or child in a violent home or community situation will focus on creating as much physical safety as possible (Bloom, 2006).

The second type of safety, central to co-regulation, is psychological safety. Psychological safety gives the person the confidence that you will respect their feelings and emotional wellbeing. This safety emerges from the trust we establish through our strength of character, consistent support, and follow-through. A psychologically safe relationship directly challenges the belief born out of trauma that all people are dangerous (Herman, 1997).

Promoting physical and psychological safety is one of the guiding principles of Pretreatment. It is based on the development of a trusting relationship, while respecting and upholding the person's sense of autonomy. When our resources and referrals improve physical safety, a spirit of partnership, compassion, and acceptance provides focus areas for building and maintaining psychological safety. Study after study over decades finds that the most critical factor in determining service outcomes is the relationship quality between you and the person. As John Murphy (2008) states:

> Research has consistently indicated that a positive person-counselor bond, or "alliance," is the strongest and most reliable predictor of successful outcomes.

Neurobiology

Trauma disrupts how the nervous system and brain develop and function. Let's briefly summarize and simplify the relationship between trauma and the nervous system. The prefrontal cortex, hippocampus, and ventral vagal nerve support executive functioning, including emotional regulation, memory formation, language, cognitive functioning, social engagement, and medical health. Repeated trauma results in these areas becoming less active and even physically smaller.

Conversely, the parts of the nervous system associated with anxiety, depression, fight, flight, and freeze trauma responses become more active and physically more prominent. These findings support the trauma-informed mantra to avoid asking, "What is wrong with this person?" and instead inquire, "What happened to this person?" The neurobiological injury of trauma accounts for many of the struggles of those we serve. The good news is that the brain changes throughout life and the right resource, support, and therapy can heal this physical injury.

The paradigm shift in neurobiology will forever change how we understand ourselves as human beings. Until the last couple of years, professionals had to assume how trauma impacted the people they helped. We applied the research but could not assess trauma's impact on nervous system health. We also hoped that our interventions and resources helped heal the injuries left over by trauma.

The paradigm now allows professionals to measure this impact with a biometric called heart rate variability (HRV). Since Steven Porges, the creator of the Polyvagal Theory, started using HRV in the 1960s, it has become the gold standard in research for measuring the stress response and the mind and body's ability to handle or recover from stress and trauma. Recent technological advancement has brought neurobiology out of the laboratory setting and is an effective tool to measure how interventions help people heal. Neurobiology is now a paradigm shift of both knowledge and practice (Bennett, 2022; Khazan, 2019; Porges, 2009)

Although HRV brings neurobiology into our daily work, we still need analogies to communicate the complexity of the brain and nervous systems. I developed a simple cup analogy to help people understand how distress and trauma affect their thoughts, feelings, and behaviors (Bennett, 2018; Ogden et al., 2006; Siegel, 2011).

The cup analogy has two parts; the first is the size of the cup. The bigger the cup, the more resilient we are to the effects of stress and the longer it takes to go into an extreme stress response. Factors such as self-confidence, healthy relationships, mindfulness, healthy eating habits, age, and exercise increase our cup size.

Conversely, unhealthy foods and sleep, long-term distress from poverty, unresolved trauma, traumatic brain injuries, drug use, struggle with employment or school, and unhealthy relationships decrease the size of the cup. Unfortunately, many people participating in services have a limited biological ability to handle stress due to trauma and intense distress. While not a reflection on them as people or even something they have much control over, most of our clients come in with small cups that quickly fill with stress, resulting in disruptive behaviors.

Typically, the capacity of the cup stays consistent over time if we do not experience significant life changes. The exception to this rule is trauma. The overwhelming nature of trauma reduces capacity quickly, and if healing does not occur, it can keep capacity low over long periods of time (Siegel, 2007; Siegel, 2011).

The second component of this analogy concerns the water in the cup. The water represents stress in our bodies at any given time. While the cup analogy helps show the accumulative effects of stress, we can describe a traumatic event as dropping your cup into a bucket full of water, where the amount of stress immediately overwhelms all ability to cope.

Ideally, when our cups start to fill, we realize our rising stress level and apply coping skills. Unfortunately, many in services carry the neurobiological wounds of trauma and never develop the necessary coping skills to prevent behaviors that might get them kicked out of programs, lose friends and family support, or lead to involvement in the criminal justice system.

The window of tolerance will help us understand how distress affects our thinking and behaviors. The space between the top of the cup and the water level represents the tolerance window. When we have adequate space between the water level in our cup and the top, we can assess our executive functions, including emotional regulation, memory formation, language, cognitive functioning, and social engagement (Stanley, 2021; Ogden et al., 2006).

Take a moment to appreciate the problematic biological and psychological situations in which many people we serve live their lives. Due to past trauma, they only have a small window of tolerance. Also, think of the amount of daily stress many people face. Homelessness, violence, poverty, food scarcity, and stigma quickly overwhelm what limited capacity leads to a life lived on the edge of their window of tolerance.

Again, the five guiding principles of Pretreatment help apply our evolving understanding of the role of stress and trauma on executive functions. In Pretreatment, the focus is on the person and not the problem. Much of Jay's writing provides an effective means of serving folks with complex trauma and multiple needs who are often mistakenly labeled and stigmatized as hard to serve and non-compliant. We work to build a strong relationship that helps us conceptualize how we can best help this person. Pretreatment also challenges us to structure our intake and onboarding processes in a way that does not add a great deal of stress to the person's already full cup, minimizing the likelihood of fight/flight responses and thereby enhancing the engagement process.

Finally, a person-centered relationship can provide the safe psychological space to engage the prefrontal cortex and more reflective responses to challenging situations. Once a trusting relationship with a common language is achieved, it sets the table for crisis/opportunity intervention. This may be needed to address instability and potentially unsafe fight/flight behaviors due to the person's window of tolerance closing or their cup beginning to overflow. Or as Jay (Levy, 2013, p. 66) states:

> ...clients will go in and out of crisis when their normal ways of coping are no longer effective at providing balance and adaptation to their current environment or circumstance. It is during these critical time periods that a trusting relationship paired with a common language can be the doorway to consider new possibilities and action, as opposed to continued inaction and apathy.

Motivational Interviewing

The trauma-informed nature of Pretreatment helped me easily apply it to my thinking on how we bring people into services and build relationships. Jay's attention to how Pretreatment *utilizes stages of change and Motivational Interviewing techniques to facilitate positive change* (Levy, 2021) allowed me to integrate its approaches into how I teach and write about Motivational Interviewing (MI). Miller and Rollnick (2023) state:

> Motivational interviewing is a particular way to talk to people about change and growth to strengthen their own motivation and commitment.

Both Pretreatment and MI focus a great deal of attention on engagement, which has two levels. First is successfully engaging or onboarding people into services. This type of engagement has crucial administrative and relational aspects (Levy, 2021, pp.19-35; Bennett, 2017). In fact, Pretreatment provides a guide via the stages Relationship Formation from Pre-engagement to the Contracting process for services in an effort to develop person-centered relationships, assessments and interventions.

The second type of engagement speaks to the person's investment in making complex life changes. Motivation strengthens or wanes depending on various relational, environmental, and personal factors. In MI, we help people contemplate and resolve these barriers to improve their lives and situations.

We can do several things to promote engagement. These strategies include concentrating on hope and positivity, desire and goals, importance, and expectations. Focusing on these strategies increases motivation and the self-efficacy needed to move through the stages of change (Miller & Rollnick, 2012).

Hope and Positivity: Hope for a better future and the ability of your services to help a person realize that future becomes a source of motivation for the person. Suppose the person does not believe you will help them make tomorrow better than today. In that case, they will likely invest little energy or effort into your relationships or services.

Positive emotions and relationships are essential, especially for people with traumatic pasts. Pretreatment promotes engagement through prioritizing a positive and strength-based helping relationship that avoids re-traumatization. Using Pretreatment relationship strategies helps the person start to see themself, their relationships, and their world in a new light.

Desire and Goals: Some people come in with a desire to change, while others might wish to stay the same but are experiencing external pressures to change. Identifying and increasing desire to change and helping the person establish goals are critical to the planning process of MI. The more a person desires change and views us as a partner in the change, the greater their engagement. Establishing a set of goals and a path forward increases engagement even further. Pretreatment allows the professional to identify where the person is, create a common language, and gently introduce future-oriented conversations concerning goals (Levy, 2000; Miller & Rollnick, 2012).

Importance: The more important something is, the more engaged someone will be with an issue or change. Importance relates to a person's desire, reason, and need to change. Most people are dealing with many issues. Addressing changes that the person sees as more significant will build both confidence and motivation. Pretreatment's person-centered approach helps the professional identify what is important to the person and start there without pressure to immediately force organizational or system goals on the person (Miller & Rollnick, 2012).

Expectations: Psychological safety increases when reality matches established expectations. It also struggles when reality fails to meet expectations. Shared expectations about your role, the boundaries around this role, the person's responsibilities, and the overall nature of the relationship structure the helping relationship for success. The more a person understands the expectations, the less likely it is that they will feel threatened and become disengaged (Miller & Rollnick, 2012).

Pretreatment provides the time to build a strong relationship and define the role of the person and professional. Many people with untreated trauma histories struggle in relationships because their trauma taught them that people, especially those in power, hurt you. Boundaries structure the expectations of all healthy relationships. A relational focus early on in the engagement process allows the professional to take the time to strengthen the relational roles and dynamics.

MI also warns us of the four main engagement traps: assessment, premature focus, labeling, and chatting. If not avoided, all may lead to disengagement, resulting in decreased motivation and possibly persons dropping out of services altogether. If the professional and the system they work in follow the five guiding principles and ten guidelines for outreach counseling, they will avoid these traps.

Assessment Trap: Assessments, including intakes, bio-psychosocial evaluations, mental status examinations, standardized tests, and medical histories, can derail engagement if conducted too early in the relationship. So many clients over the years expressed their frustration with doing "one more assessment." As discussed above, the Pretreatment framework helps us minimize the chance of re-traumatization while avoiding this trap (Miller & Rollnick, 2012).

Premature Focus Trap: Premature focus entails jumping to solutions before establishing the partnership. Focusing on problem-solving before the person is ready will cause discord and possibly resistance, which is a clue for you to slow down and meet the person where they are in the stages of change. We will look at this trap in more detail below and how Pretreatment helps us to craft our approach to avoid this trap.

Labeling Trap: Society and the helping professions have created volumes of labels. While these can help guide treatment, they are often detrimental to the person. Having someone accept a label has few or no positive benefits for behavioral change. Being labeled homeless, borderline, HIV-positive, or addict can negatively affect the person and their motivation (Miller & Rollnick, 2012).

Pretreatment's focus on creating a common language helps people understand that they are not their diagnosis or label. Labels can dramatically increase defensiveness and bring forth resistance. A person experiencing homelessness is much more than their housing situation, someone with bipolar disorder is not just their mood swings, and a formerly incarcerated person is not their criminal history. We must ensure we handle labeling carefully and avoid it whenever possible (Miller & Rollnick, 2012). As Jay (Levy, 2010, p. 62) states:

> If the worker continues to think mainly in terms of treatment, illness, and symptoms, then the opportunity of really hearing and responding on a human level is bypassed.

Chatting Trap: Finally, we should avoid the chatting trap. Chatting creates a situation without focus or direction to guide the conversation.

Chatting is an easy trap because many people do not have people in their lives who listen.

Most people want to feel they have accomplished something. Since we hold the role of expert, the person may assume that our chatting is part of the process and will help them achieve their goals. However, if the interaction is not structured, most people will eventually get frustrated at the lack of improvement in their situation. This frustration can lead to decreased motivation and disengagement (Miller & Rollnick, 2012).

The Spirit of MI is one critical bridge between Pretreatment, trauma-informed care, and MI. The Spirit of MI provides a foundational philosophy for implementing strategies that help people change and heal. The Spirit of MI includes partnership, empowerment, acceptance, and compassion.

Spirit of Partnership: Miller and Rollnick (2012) state: "Your purpose is to understand the life before you, to see the world through this person's eyes rather than superimposing your vision."

Often, from our perspective, what the person needs to do seems obvious: for example, they need to stop abusing drugs, take their life-saving HIV medication, or leave their abusive partner. The partnership entails putting judgment aside. It challenges us to create an understanding of the person in the context of their situation, including their struggles with trauma.

Pretreatment is all about creating the time and space to develop this partnership. Pretreatment challenges us to observe, respect personal space, assess safety, offer essential needed items, and listen to the client's language (Levy, 2000). All these approaches build a working partnership with the person and overcome engagement traps (Miller & Rollnick, 2012). Jay (Levy, 2018, p. 219) states:

> The counselor is challenged to work with, not against, people's strengths, values, and meaning. This means listening carefully, and "tuning in" to the person's universe of language, while letting go of our "program speak" in favor of individualization.

Spirit of Empowerment: The second Spirit of MI is empowerment. Empowerment is our ability to bring out the wisdom that lies within the person. The goal here is to help people regain the strength and confidence often lost in traumatic experiences and struggles in the past.

In MI, people are the experts on themselves. To empower the person to be the expert on their condition, they need to voice the reason and need for change.

Working in the Spirit of Empowerment, we strategically help the person to hear their voice. As the expert, the person is talking more than half the time. It is hard for the person to hear their voice when the professional does all the talking (Miller & Rollnick, 2023).

Spirit of Acceptance: Acceptance helps the person find a sense of worth. Unfortunately, people with trauma histories often struggle to reestablish a positive view of themselves due to past struggles and trauma. Trauma can leave a person feeling they deserved the abuse or were responsible for it. Even though this thinking has no logic, this feeling immobilizes the person on their journey of change and healing (Miller & Rollnick, 2012).

Change and healing require someone to feel they are worthy of improvement. If the person cannot find a sense of self-value, they will also not find the motivation for change. Many people come in with a history of trauma, pain, and suffering, leaving them with a negative view of themselves, their relationships, and the world. Your task is to find the good in the person and reflect this value to them. MI is a strengths-based approach, meaning it recognizes that if a change is to occur, it will happen because of the person's strengths and the support of the professional (Miller & Rollnick, 2012).

Empathy is a crucial aspect of acceptance. Miller and Rollnick (2012) define empathy not only as *an ability to understand another's frame of reference* but continue to make a critical point that it is also *the conviction that it is worthwhile to do so*. Empathy is essential because, without empathy, we cannot build the necessary trust and safety with the person that is critical for healing and growth. Pretreatment shifts the focus from collecting information to understanding the person.

The final approach to acceptance is autonomy. Autonomy is the acknowledgment that freedom of choice increases the possibility for change. Pretreatment allows the professional to get to know the person and their motivations so that we can effectively provide options based on available resources. In fact, the Pretreatment focus of the engagement process is to develop trust, respect autonomy, and construct a common language to inspire ongoing dialogue leading to chosen goals reflective of the person's words, ideas and values.

We bring our expertise on resources and help create potential steps to realize the change, but the person is the one who acts to achieve the change. Many people may not see that they have any power to make choices in their situation. MI and Pretreatment provide us with structures to bring our expertise and present the person with options that may have been previously unknown to them (Levy, 2000; Miller & Rollnick, 2012).

Motivation is something someone has inside them at any given moment. It fluctuates with the many variables in the person's life, but regardless, it comes from within them. The more they understand that they have a choice and the capacity to change, the more likely they will take the first steps toward change. Reinforcing autonomy helps the person regain some of the power lost in the traumatic experience that can lead to a life trapped in harmful habits and addiction (Miller & Rollnick, 2012).

Spirit of Compassion: The fourth Spirit of MI is compassion. Miller and Rollnick (2012) use the concept of compassion very specifically. They are not talking about a kind of feeling or experience of sympathy. They do not mean to "suffer with." They say, "*To be compassionate is to actively promote the other's welfare, to give priority to the other's needs.*"

At its core, compassion is the commitment to what is in the person's best interest. MI and Pretreatment teach that providing support works better than confrontation. Support is especially critical for people with trauma histories, who often have trouble trusting people and systems. Compassion means having our hearts in the right place to serve others, not in a manipulative way to try to get compliance, but in an honest way that leads to trust and support. It requires patience and the understanding that difficult change takes time and is vital to establishing relationships that improve outcomes.

Stages of Change and the MI Hill

Pretreatment fits perfectly into the stages of change and provides practical approaches and tools to navigate the most difficult early stages. James Prochaska and Carlo DiClemente developed the Stages of Change model during the late 1970s and early 1980s. This model challenged how people thought about change and helped inspire the creation of MI. Prochaska and DiClemente demonstrated that change is not an event but a process. If we can identify where the person is in the stages, we can implement strategies to help them move to the next stage and one step closer to their change goals (Prochaska, DiClemente, & Norcross, 1992).

Understanding neuroscience and trauma helps deepen understanding of Pretreatment's importance in supporting people through the stages of change. The brain becomes more efficient by creating habits based on past experiences and repeated behaviors. Unfortunately, many habits people develop to survive trauma, homelessness, and other life situations prevent them from succeeding in other environments.

The good news is that the discovery of the brain's neuroplasticity means old habits and unhealthy behaviors can change with time and focus. Neuroscience has shown that the brain is constantly changing. The ability of the brain to change is called neuroplasticity. Neuroplasticity refers to changes in brain structure due to changes in the environment, behavior, thinking, feeling, and experience. While the brain can change to support positive behavior change, it takes time for new structures to emerge.

You can think of going to the gym to increase the size of the biceps. This takes many repetitions of curls. Similarly, it takes many repetitions for a new behavior to become a healthy habit (Schwartz & Begley, 2002).

"Meeting the person where they are at" is central to stages of change, MI, trauma-informed care, harm reduction, and Pretreatment. In the context of behavior change, MI research demonstrates the importance of identifying which stage the person is in at that moment and crafting our communication precisely to the challenges of that stage. Resistance is evoked when the professional starts planning or advocating for action while the person is still contemplating.

Unfortunately, success in many systems entails the professional getting the person to act differently. Changing behaviors to succeed in a housing program, stopping using substances, achieving medical adherence, and other such changes are the metrics by which our success gets measured. Action is the fourth stage of change and depends on the person successfully working through the pre-contemplation, contemplation, and preparation stages, each with its unique set of challenges. From a neurobiological perspective, each stage strengthens the structures in the brain that support the healthier habit or behavior.

Pretreatment provides a space to meet people in the early stages of change, minimizing the chance for resistance. Even when implemented perfectly, Pretreatment and MI will not guarantee rapid change. It will promote the most efficient path to action, even if the person needs several months to get through the first three stages.

It is important to remember that motivation is not a trait but a state that changes for various reasons. Someone is not motivated or unmotivated. Motivation, like other emotional states, can strengthen or weaken due to everything from a strengthening relationship with the professionals to a lousy night's sleep.

Miller and Rollnick (2012) provide the analogy of the MI hill to bring together change talk, MI skills, and the stages of change. On one side of the hill is preparatory change talk, which helps people progress through the pre-contemplation and contemplation stages. In the hill analogy, preparatory change talk is the upward climb, which can be slow and arduous.

Fig. 2-1: The MI Hill (Miller and Rollnick)

At the beginning of the change journey, there is no momentum and little insight, self-confidence is lacking, and motivation is nonexistent. It is important not to become frustrated with the realities of pre-contemplation. Recognizing that a person is in this stage permits us to be patient and non-judgmental and to focus on building the relationship while avoiding being the one pushing for change to happen. Maintaining patience might be hard when you see the negative consequences of the person's behavior on themselves and others. However, pushing them into the planning or action stages will lead to frustration and resistance.

Once people consider change seriously, they move from the pre-contemplation stage into contemplation. In this stage, they acknowledge that a problem exists. For people with traumatic pasts, this insight often carries an elevated level of anxiety, shame, and guilt. This emotional reaction can be extreme enough to push the person into denial and back into pre-contemplation. It is essential to spend time supporting and helping the person process their emotional response during contemplation.

The journey up the MI hill is often rough and slow going, as the person fights through all the self-doubt and external barriers that have prevented them from making the change in the past. Pretreatment proves its value in these first two stages. Jay's approach provides the professional with a set of approaches and tools to communicate and engage people when motivation is still emerging and social support is so important. Pretreatment helps further increase the efficiency of the journey up the MI Hill. As Jay (Levy, 2021, p. 94) states:

> Many of the people we serve are afraid to hope. They have experienced so much trauma, disappointment, failure, and mistreatment by others that the sense of shame, guilt and anger that accompany their fears appears too insurmountable to even begin conversations on what's possible. For these folks, our approach is relationship based, more focused on Harm Reduction and Crisis Intervention as we develop a Common Language that slowly aligns itself with the words and concepts to help the person contemplate the need for change.

Pretreatment helps the professional and client identify their desire, ability, reason, and need (DARN) for change. DARN is where the energy and thinking about the change elicits motivation.

Desire is the extent to which the person wants the change to happen. When a person is early in the change process, desire often focuses on continuing old behaviors. Behaviors that are hard to change or stop altogether usually entail giving up something one likes to do.

Drinking helps with stress. Taking a new medication may be undesirable because of side effects. Exercising every morning means getting up earlier. Leaving an abusive partner may mean facing danger and uncertainty. Ambivalence about change is natural and you should not push too quickly if the desire is not there (Miller & Rollnick, 2012).

Ability is the person's self-perceived confidence to achieve change. No one likes to fail. If people do not think they can do something, they probably will not do it. We can assist by helping them identify past successes and strengths they might not have seen in themselves. As confidence and self-efficacy build, the chance the person will act increases. Believing one can change is a signal that change is possible (Miller & Rollnick, 2012).

Reason often comes from internal or external motivators, especially if there is no desire for change. Reason is the person's purpose for considering the change. For example, they must stop getting high because it violates their parole. A stated reason does not imply ability or desire (Miller & Rollnick, 2012).

Need is the importance and urgency the person feels concerning the change. An example might be that the person must stop using drugs immediately or social services could take their child out of the home. Identifying need often involves external consequences looming for the person if they do not change. While need can be a significant motivator to preparation and action, it does not imply that the person has confidence in their ability or imply that there is a desire to make the change (Miller & Rollnick, 2012).

Preparatory change talk, like motivation itself, is dynamic. In one session, a person might talk about their internal desire and the external need to change, but they might lack the confidence or ability to take action. At the next session, they might have more confidence, but the desire might have disappeared, and the change might have lost some importance. This fluctuation is natural; the key to preparatory change talk is to spend time discussing wherever it lies on that day.

MI challenges us to evoke preparatory change talk and use active listening skills to help the person contemplate the change. The most powerful finding in MI research is that the more the person talks about the change, the more likely the change will occur. Our goal, especially in the Pretreatment context, is to increase preparatory change talk. (Miller & Rollnick, 2012)

Harm Reduction

Too often, the requirements of the program or system dictate the agenda, providing little room to customize services and resources around a person's unique needs. This rigid method of delivering services leads to disengagement and poor outcomes. Luckily, pretreatment and harm reduction provide a different philosophical foundation for creating agendas.

At its core, harm reduction allows us and our programs to meet people where they are in their journey to change. Harm reduction fits in comfortably with Pretreatment and the other paradigms presented in this chapter. The fourth principle of Pretreatment is to *Promote Safety* based on crisis intervention and harm reduction strategies. Research demonstrates that harm-reduction approaches have succeeded where traditional methods have struggled (Marlatt, Larimer, & Witkiewitz, 2012).

Traditional models of services often detract from focus and lead to disengagement. The moral model perceives behaviors as right or wrong, good or evil, punishing people who engage in these behaviors. The criminal model identifies specific actions as crimes. The disease model looks at certain behaviors as symptoms of a sickness. The cure for the disease often entails complete abstinence or eliminating the behavior. As discussed earlier, trauma takes away a positive view of self. These programs can reinforce this thinking by adding negative labels or messages that people quickly and entirely internalize (Marlatt, Larimer, & Witkiewitz, 2012).

In contrast, harm reduction relies on compassionate pragmatism, which accepts that negative behaviors will always exist in society. This philosophy does not mean we view every behavior or action as proper or ethical. Instead, we acknowledge that they exist and realize that the less damage they inflict, the better for the person and the community (Roe, 2005).

Harm reduction is trauma-informed, challenging us to search for the deeper causes of harmful behavior. It goes beyond placing blame on the individual and identifies the social causes of the condition, which for most people include trauma. This recognition of societal causes creates new possibilities for prevention and community interventions that address the person's struggles and the systematic causes leading to those struggles. Harm-reduction approaches, like trauma-informed methods, challenge us to shift the question from "What is wrong with you?" to "What happened to you?"

In harm-reduction, Pretreatment, MI, and trauma-informed approaches, the problem does not define the person. While the behavior is harmful, the person has inherent value beyond their behaviors. Harm reduction challenges us to meet the person where they are in their stage of change and does not put unrealistic restrictions on services. Instead, the professional collaborates with the person to set a shared agenda for services because for lasting change to occur, the motivation for change must come from the person (Miller & Rollnick, 2012).

Compassion is limited in systems that see the person as immoral or sick. If, as a society, we believe the person's problems result because of something wrong with them, and we do not acknowledge other societal factors and how past trauma is contributing to the situation, it is easy to place blame and point fingers, but that does not improve results. When the person internalizes this blame, it is even harder to find motivation for change and can lead to re-traumatization and disengagement.

Structuring programs and delivery services based on harm reduction and Pretreatment helps ensure that the Spirit of MI is at the center of our work. Harm reduction, Pretreatment, and MI have partnerships, compassion, and acceptance at their heart. Putting these approaches together creates a service atmosphere ideal for people with traumatic histories to engage in their change and heal from past pain and suffering.

Harm reduction challenges society to prioritize the person's and community's long-term best interests. Giving a person who injects heroin clean needles might have a small upfront cost, but compared to the enormous cost of HIV or hepatitis treatment, the price of a clean needle is next to nothing. Needle exchange, free birth control, housing first, and other harm-reduction programs reduce long-term damage with less expensive and more effective interventions (World Health Organization, 2004; Miller & Rollnick, 2012).

Taking the view that a person is immoral or sick makes it easy to treat them as having little worth, which goes against the Spirit of MI. This attitude or belief leads to a directing and confrontational style of interaction that pays little attention to the expertise the person can bring to helping themselves or their situation. Instead of resulting in the desired change, these interventions more often create resistance. In harm reduction, Pretreatment, and MI, the person is a partner with control of their services and treatment. This empowerment helps them see themselves as experts with the necessary answers to improve their situation and wellbeing (Miller & Rollnick, 2012).

Few people access services when their lives are running smoothly. They do so when they are struggling with the consequences of negative behaviors and are coping with adverse life situations. Access to services is either a high threshold or a low threshold. Many traditional models apply the high-threshold model, asking people to meet preconditions before accessing services. For example, to receive drug and alcohol treatment services, many programs require that people maintain sobriety throughout treatment. This approach is high-threshold access to services.

Here is where Pretreatment thrives. It lowers any threshold and focuses the professional on relationship-building regardless of behaviors. Pretreatment provides a structure and framework for programs and systems attempting to integrate harm reduction practices. Low threshold harm-reduction programs do more than provide resources to increase safety and lower healthcare costs. When viewed through a Pretreatment lens, these are relationship-based programs providing needed items that promote engagement, ongoing support, crisis intervention, and the promise of productive dialogue facilitating the contemplation process of positive change.

As with moral and disease models, harm-reduction programs often have abstinence as the end goal. The difference is that harm-reduction programs have a low-threshold approach to care. In low-threshold environments, we meet the person where they are in life and do not place behavioral requirements, like abstinence or other rigid conditions, on accessing services. This approach allows more people access to service, allows us to start working with people regardless of where they are in their change process, and works to stabilize and gradually reduce behaviors with potentially adverse consequences. A low-threshold approach treats the whole person and not just one disorder or problem, setting the stage for high levels of empathy, compassion, and engagement (Marlatt, Larimer, & Witkiewitz, 2012).

Pretreatment approaches provide tools to help focus this work and maximize results. First, the professional has an awareness and understanding of the nature and causes of certain potentially harmful behaviors. This knowledge results from learning from the stories of the people's lives, supplemented by the professional's dedication to developing trust and safety.

Second, there is a focus on enhancing coping skills to manage stressful situations. These can be frank and robust conversations surrounding behaviors with potentially harmful consequences. It might be hard at first to discuss how to use an illegal substance or have sex in safer ways, but these are necessary steps to reducing harm for the person and community.

The third is the promotion of stabilization through training in reducing harm and increasing safety. The nature of potentially harmful behaviors puts the person in dangerous situations. Injecting drugs exposes the person to a hazardous substance and might result in needle sharing and being vulnerable in unsafe social situations. Harm reduction focuses equally on increasing safety and reducing present dangers (Levy, 2021).

Finally, we can help train the person in health-promoting behaviors. Many people continue potentially harmful behaviors because abstinence seems too overwhelming. Even just one sober day a week might make the person confident enough to try two days a week. In another situation, a person who might not want to take medication for a chronic disease might be open to other healthy activities, such as improved nutrition or starting a movement practice (Marlatt, Larimer, & Witkiewitz, 2012).

Harm-reduction approaches engage people where they are in the stage of change journey, keep us aligned with the Spirit of MI, increase the opportunity for change talk to occur, and increase engagement. They also serve as a foundation along with trauma-informed methods for people to access our next topic, taking part in open dialogue and creating a shared agenda. Jay (Levy, 2018, p. 219) states:

> It is in our willingness to cross the cultural divide, and faith that an open dialogue can result in mutual understanding and goal focused work that opens the door to new possibilities. This sets the stage for healthy change. It is an opportunity for the worker and the client, as well as our systems of care to get "unstuck" by shifting their perspectives.

Conclusion

Pretreatment provides a set of philosophies and strategies to transform systems to meet the challenges and promises of these revolutionary paradigms. Meeting Jay on my professional journey has been a gift. As Neurobiology, Harm Reduction, Motivational Interviewing and Trauma-Informed Care permeate our society and understanding of human behavior, we need people like Jay to help simplify and focus our approaches to help people live better lives and address the social issues facing our communities. Pretreatment and its guiding principles of care integrates these approaches and makes them applicable and readily accessible to our daily work in the field of human service.

References

Bennett, M. S. (2017). *Connecting paradigms: A trauma-informed and neurobiological framework for motivational interviewing implementation*. Denver: A BIG Publication.

Bennett, M. S. (2018). *Talking about trauma and change: A connecting paradigms supplement*. Denver: A BIG Publication.

Bloom, S. L. (2006). Organizational stress as a barrier to trauma-sensitive change and system transformation. A white paper for National Technical Assistance Center for State Mental Health Planning (NTAC).

Bloom, S. L., & Farragher, B. (2011). *Destroying sanctuary: The crisis in human service delivery systems*. New York: Oxford University Press.

Felitti, V. J., Anda, R. F., Nordenberg, D., Williamson, D. F., Spitz, A. M., Edwards, V., Koss, M. P., & Marks, J. S. (1998). Relationship of childhood abuse and household dysfunction to many of the leading causes of death in adults: The Adverse Childhood Experiences (ACE) Study. *American Journal of Preventive Medicine, 14*(4), 245–258.

Herman, J. L. (1997). *Trauma and recovery*. New York: Basic Books.

Khazan, I. (2019). *Biofeedback and mindfulness in everyday life: Practical solutions for improving your health and performance*. New York: W. W. Norton & Company.

Levy, J. S. (2000, July-August). Homeless outreach: On the road to pretreatment alternatives. *Families in Society: The Journal of Contemporary Human Services*, 81(4), 360-368.

Levy, J. S. (2010). *Homeless narratives & pretreatment pathways: From words to housing*. Ann Arbor, MI: Loving Healing Press.

Levy, J. S. (2013). *Pretreatment guide for homeless outreach & Housing First: Helping couples, youth, and unaccompanied adults*. Ann Arbor, MI: Loving Healing Press.

Levy, J. S. with Johnson, R. (2018). *Cross-cultural dialogues on homelessness: From pretreatment strategies to psychologically informed environments*. Ann Arbor, MI: Loving Healing Press.

Levy, J. S. (2021). *Pretreatment in action: Interactive exploration of homelessness to housing stabilization*. Ann Arbor, MI: Loving Healing Press.

Marlatt, G. A., Larimer, M. E., & Witkiewitz, K. (Eds.). (2012). *Harm reduction: Pragmatic strategies for managing high-risk behaviors*. New York: Guilford Press.

Merriam-Webster (2023) https://www.merriam-webster.com/dictionary/paradigm%20shift

Miller, W. R., & Rollnick, S. (2023). *Motivational interviewing: Helping people change* (4th ed.). New York: Guilford Press.

Miller, W. R., & Rollnick, S. (2012). *Motivational interviewing: Helping people change* (3rd ed.). New York: Guilford Press.

Murphy, J. J. (2008). *Solution-focused counseling in schools* (2nd ed.). Alexandria, VA: American Counseling Assoc. http://counselingoutfitters.com/vistas/vistas08/Murphy.htm.

Ogden, P., Minton, K., & Pain, C. (2006). *Trauma and the body.* New York: W. W. Norton & Company.

Porges, S. W. (2009). The polyvagal theory: New insights into adaptive reactions of the autonomic nervous system. *Cleveland Clinic Journal of Medicine*, *76*(Supplement 2), S86–S90.

Prochaska, J. O., DiClemente, C. C., & Norcross, J. C. (1992). In search of how people change: Applications to addictive behaviors. *American Psychology* 47,1102.

Roe, G. (2005). Harm reduction as paradigm: Is better than bad good enough? *Critical Public Health*, *15*(3), 243–250.

Schwartz, J. D., & Begley, S. (2002). *The mind and the brain: Neuroplasticity and the power of mental force*. New York: HarperCollins.

Stanley, E. A. (2021). *Widen the window: Training your brain and body to thrive during stress and recover from trauma*. New York: Avery.

Substance Abuse and Mental Health Services Administration. *SAMHSA's Concept of Trauma and Guidance for a Trauma-Informed Approach*. HHS Publication No. (SMA) 14-4884. Rockville, MD: Substance Abuse and Mental Health Services Administration, 2014.

3 Dialogues Across Cultural Divides

Jay S. Levy

> Dialogue, as the encounter of those addressed to the common task of learning and acting, is broken if the parties (or one of them) lack humility. How can I dialogue if I always project ignorance onto others and never perceive my own?
>
> Paulo Freire (1970)

Introduction

Pretreatment philosophy stipulates that achieving a trusting relationship sets a strong foundation for our work, while common language construction is our main tool for crossing cultural divides. Narrative psychology and its proponents, myself included, believe that true humility begins with our presumption that the people we are trying to help are experts in their own lives (Epston & White, 1992). Therefore, the onus is on us to engage with humility by getting where they are at, as opposed to simply trying to convince them of our so-called truths and expertise.

Here, we will focus on both the importance of achieving a common language in our work with individuals and forming alliances to address systemic issues ranging from poverty and homelessness to racial and equity issues. The promise of productive dialogue is where the power for positive change lies for and with ourselves, others, and our communities.

The Art of Dialogue with Vulnerable People

Pretreatment focuses on getting person-centered with people who have experienced significant trauma and present with complex and multiple needs. These may be due to homelessness or housing instability, poverty, oppression, and/or major medical concerns, learning disabilities, addiction, mental health issues, etc. These folks may experience difficulties trusting others, deny their significant clinical issues, as well as become disaffiliated from the healthcare network and other needed resources due to stigma and the inflexibility of treatment-biased services. As a program manager, supervisor, and outreach counselor, I have witnessed on countless occasions how we can bring about positive change once we establish a working relationship that earns a person's trust and respects their sense of autonomy, as well as facilitates communication based on mutually accepted words, ideas, and values. Ultimately, fostering an initial communication that is respectful of the person's world may open the door to future productive dialogue resulting in goal-driven work defined through the lens of the client's world.

Our objective is to enter the same house of language as the client, or at least be invited to play on the mutual "playground of language" that is located between the worker's and client's houses of language[6]. Everything begins with the worker listening for the words, ideas, and values of the client and then reflecting back what is heard to make sure we are developing a real and authentic communication.

The following worker-client narrative brings to life the challenges of the Pretreatment principle of Common Language Construction and its critical importance in facilitating dialogue that upholds the sanctity of the helping relationship.

---

[6] The concepts of "House of Language" and "Playground of Language" are derived from my own hands-on practice, as well as from philosophy of language texts. Heidegger states (1971, p. 63), "Language is the House of Being" and Derrida (1976, pp. 50-59) demonstrates the use of language as a relational, creative, and playful process.

Sidney's Narrative: From the Korean War to Homelessness

During the early 1990s I provided weekly outreach counseling at a place called the Night Center in Boston, MA. We called the Night Center the "street with walls" as it was a late-night drop-in with no cots; people were literally strewn across the floor or would fight over access to available floor space. The lucky ones would sometimes find a chair to sit in. People showed up in droves to escape the outdoor elements and get a snack and coffee. They could come and go as they pleased, which afforded a quick return to the streets just in case they felt too enclosed, anxious, or bothered by others, or if they needed a quick hit of hard liquor or a fix to get by for the night, etc.

This is where I first met Sidney, an African-American male in his mid-60s who appeared quite isolated despite residing in such a crowded space. He sat quietly on a wooden chair located in the corner of the room facing the wall. He was wearing a Boston Red Sox baseball cap and almost disappeared beneath his many layers of baggy soiled clothes. During my first couple of attempts to engage him in initial conversation (Pre-engagement Stage), Sidney simply gave one-word answers and provided little or no eye contact. Upon my third approach, I offered Sidney a need-item of new socks and he accepted my offer with a soft thank you, but still did not partake in any further communication. This was a small step forward, though we remained in early engagement as we had not yet gotten to the point of a welcomed ongoing communication.

When doing outreach, during the pre-engagement and early engagement stages, part of our reflective practice is to consider safety, acute medical and behavioral health concerns, as well as cultural considerations or divides that may impact the engagement process. Sidney's mental status was hard to discern as he was quite guarded, though my early impression was of notable lethargy, and him being unable or not wanting to attend to his hygiene, which could indicate medical and/or behavioral health-related concerns such as depression.

However, these types of initial quasi-clinical assessments often miss the mark and are not all that helpful prior to understanding the person's narrative and scope of experience. Our hope is to achieve a person-centered, goal-driven relationship that is responsive to the client's culture, values, and aspirations, as opposed to being primarily focused on their diagnosis and deficits. This entails crossing cultural divides and eventually partaking in productive dialogue that respects the expertise of the client in their own world, while unleashing the expertise of the worker in a joint effort to attain positive life change.

In this case, it was evident that Sidney was an impoverished person of color and an elder (60s), while I was a middle-class white male in my 30s. So, Sidney's reservations to engage could have been due to cultural differences, experiences of evident oppression by white society, as well as his past negative encounters with younger men. In this regard, the onus is on the outreach counselor to take on the challenge of crossing cultural divides by promoting a greater sense of safety and trust, while being careful not to come across as impatient, authoritative or controlling. This means respecting the world of the client and preparing oneself to speak to their concerns, needs and wants, while not personalizing their understandable sense of caution, distrust, and/or anger.

Prior to the next round of outreach, I meditated further upon the cultural divides that were most evident between Sidney and me. I soon realized that Sidney reminded me of my very first client who went by the moniker of "Old Man Ray."[7] Ray was a World War II Veteran, and he taught me a great deal about the value of elders being able to share their stories and wisdom with younger folks. This reflection also made me wonder if Sidney was the right age for serving in the military during Vietnam or perhaps stationed somewhere prior. Keeping all this in mind, I was ready for my next attempt at outreach and engagement, though I now had a growing curiosity about his narrative.

During the next round of outreach at the Night Center, I approached Sidney and said, "Did you have a chance to try on the socks?" He pointed toward his ankle and pulled up his trousers to show me. I responded, "Looks good Sidney! Since our last meeting I was reflecting about your age and wondering if you had ever served in the military?" He nodded yes. I continued, "You are not alone, I've met quite a few folks without homes who have served in the military... When did you

---

[7] The reader may want to acquaint themselves with Old Man Ray's Narrative, which was first published in the book *Homeless Narratives & Pretreatment Pathways: From Words to Housing* (Levy, 2010).

serve and what branch?" Sidney responded with improved eye contact, "I served during the Korean War and was a pilot in the Air Force." I immediately responded with a sense of awe and wonder, "Wow… I am so appreciative of your service. You are the first person that I ever met who served in Korea. It must have really been something to be a pilot in the US Air Force during the Korean War!" For the first time, Sidney smiled, nodded, and said, "I have my share of stories from the war. It was a difficult time, but I made many friends and we made it through together." This opened the door for our first extended conversation and many more would soon follow.

We had begun to establish a Common Language based on Sidney's vast experience and expertise in the military. It is important to note that I always followed his cues as to what was welcomed on the "playground of language." Even in terms of my initial questions, I was careful to inquire whether he had ever served in the Military as opposed to asking if he was currently a Veteran. This is because some folks do not consider themselves a Veteran unless they experienced combat and/or had an honorable discharge. In this case, part of forming a common language was to understand military culture including that many may believe that a certain branch of service ranks above another branch of service. This is why I offered a general question regarding what branch, as well as when and where he served, as I did not want to appear to be pre-judging his service. Sydney was the one in charge and I did my best to learn from his experience and respect his particular use of language.

The first stage of Common Language Construction is to *understand* a person's words, ideas, and values (see Table 3-1 on p. 59, *Stage 1: Understand Language*). In this manner, much was accomplished before sharing my own expertise as an outreach counselor. It is all about Engagement and finding my way into Sidney's world to work on mutual goals, rather than relying on my preconceived outreach agenda of quickly bridging him into the world of treatment. Or, in other words, we had entered the early stages of Engagement and Common Language Construction, as evidenced by our now welcomed conversations, but had not yet contracted for services, nor had we utilized his language to construct the goals that could best guide our work. We had established some trust and regular outreach meetings that set the stage for goal setting and productive dialogue.

During our next encounter, I asked Sidney if he was aware of some of the Veteran's benefits offered on the Federal level through Veteran's Affairs (VA benefits), or on the State level (Chapter 115 benefits[8]), whether it be income, shelter, or even subsidized housing . Sidney gave a deep sigh, and shared, "I never had time for that. When I first came back from the war I stayed on mission. I was there to support other Veterans who were dealing with the effects of combat, but my efforts were not appreciated, so I decided to go it alone." I responded, "So you felt unappreciated despite your best efforts to be of help?" Sidney then said with notable anger, "More than that… I was mistreated due to being a black man in the USA! Sure, it was fine when I served during the war, but when I came back, nobody gave a fuck!" After a short pause, he sighed and said, "That's how I ended up here." I responded, "I hear that you've been mistreated because of the color of your skin and betrayed. I know that you deserve better than this. You served our country at great risk to your own wellbeing. We all owe you a debt for your service." Sidney responded emphatically, "Fuck yeah!" so I continued, "Frankly, I am in awe of you being a pilot in the Air Force and can't stand that you're forced to live here. There is a local Veteran's shelter that serves the Boston area and if you let me, I'd really like to see if we can get you that and some of the other Veteran's benefits you deserve!" Upon hearing that I shared his moral outrage, Sidney nodded in agreement.

We proceeded to getting the information needed, so I could see if he qualified for Veteran Services and the local Vets shelter. This meant that we needed to apply for his DD214 (discharge papers from the military) to prove that he had served. Sidney stated that he was interested in receiving healthcare, affordable housing and cash benefits and I explained that we could follow up with Veterans Affairs and State level services. I also knew that if we ran into any problems there, we could still apply for Social Security as he was of retirement age.

Back at the office I gave Jack, who is our local VSO (Veterans Services Officer), a call. My dialogue with Jack and my past clients (e.g., Old Man Ray) had taught me a great deal about Veteran's culture, their language and what they valued, as well as the rules and policies of the

---

[8] First established by the Massachusetts Legislature during the US Civil War in 1861.

VA (Veterans Affairs). Jack sent in the DD214 and we soon heard back. Sidney had an honorable discharge.

I quickly shared the good news with Sidney that he was indeed fully eligible for Veteran's resources and services. We were now squarely in the contracting stage of engagement and had begun working on his goals of attaining a safe place to sleep via the Vets shelter, as well as applying for affordable housing, healthcare and financial benefits. Sidney began to open up more and shared that he had been homeless for ten years and now had some significant pain and discomfort with his feet. I also observed over an extended time period that he had symptoms of depression (i.e., lethargy, reported helplessness and hopelessness, depressed affect, unkempt hygiene, etc.) and that he was imbibing nips of vodka daily. I referred Sydney to both the Veteran's Shelter and to our local Healthcare for the Homeless Nurse for foot soaks, as well as further medical and mental health attention and evaluation. Fortunately, he accepted both referrals as they were directly in response to his stated needs to receive safe shelter and healthcare. We appeared to be on the right track, before going on a major detour.

After referring Sidney to the Veteran's shelter, we attended an intake meeting there and, to my chagrin, the shelter staff requested that he sign a CORI (Criminal Offender Records Information). Unfortunately, information derived from CORI checks often derail access to needed resources. Nevertheless, this was required in advance to establish eligibility for successful placement into subsidized Veteran's Housing Programs. Sidney immediately got very agitated and abruptly ended the intake meeting. Later, back at the Night Center, Sidney sat quietly getting the first of several foot soaks by the Health Care for the Homeless nurse. He then shared with me that being required to sign a CORI was just another example of people mistreating him. Sidney said in a sad and angry tone, "See, I told you! I am stuck in a living hell and they are just looking for ways to deny me!"

For the moment, our progress had hit a significant barrier, one constructed of past traumas, oppression, loss, and rejection in combination with a rigid and biased system of care. This also raised the very real possibility that there was more to Sidney's story than met the eye.

My experience is that most single adult males without homes have been arrested and/or have been unjustly accused of crimes by authorities.

This is particularly substantial among people of color. In fact, according to the NAACP Criminal Justice Fact Sheet (2023), one out of every three Black males born today in the USA can expect to be sentenced to prison, compared 1 out 6 Latino males; and only 1 out of 17 white males. Another telling statistic is that a Black person is five times more likely to be stopped by police without just cause than a white person. When criminal record (CORI) checks are routinely done to see if people meet the eligibility for resources and services, it is not unusual for an adult male experiencing homelessness, and in particular a person of color, to be denied access. This is one of the many systemic issues that maintains the status quo of homelessness.

Approximately one week later, Sidney and I met at a nearby park to discuss the current standstill. I was careful to join with Sidney by empathizing with him as he expressed his long history of mistreatment. I also spoke to my disappointment that they didn't just give him a shelter bed, rather than asking for a CORI to be signed. I shared (further joining and universalizing the issue) that he wasn't alone in not wanting to sign the CORI and wondered if he was worried about what they might find. Sidney responded that he wasn't sure, but he had been unjustly hassled by the police in the past and wouldn't be surprised if there was a charge on his record from the distant past. I explained to Sidney that *together* we could take a stand against injustice and at the same time try to get him the resources and services that he deserved to move things forward. I then reframed the offer of him signing a CORI as something we could review *together*, before sharing it with anyone. If there were any charges, then *we* could figure out the best way to proceed by consulting with a lawyer and asking for accommodation based on his past military service, advanced age, and current state of homelessness. He understood that this was all part of *our mission* for fair and just treatment. In response, Sidney signed the CORI and agreed for us to continue the work of achieving his goals (healthcare, housing, and benefits).

This was a critical meeting with Sidney and the positive outcome depended upon our past work of building a trusting relationship, the ongoing development and use of a Common Language, as well as joining with the client on a defined "mission" to seek "justice" and "fair treatment." This Pretreatment approach upheld the person-centered relationship as opposed to entrenching cultural divides between Sidney and the worker (me). Our Common Language was primarily constructed from Sidney's experiences of being a war veteran, as well as his cultural and reported experiences of mistreatment, injustice and oppression as a person of color. I now better understood what Sidney meant by his use of these terms (his said and unsaid[9]). This, in turn, enabled me to utilize his words and ideas effectively in my communications with him (see Table 3 on p. 59 - *Stage 2: Utilize Language*).

Unfortunately, Sidney's CORI showed that he had a warrant out for his arrest. He was charged with being in possession of burglary tools approximately twelve years prior and was a no-show for his court date. As promised, we followed up with a free legal consult. We were advised that the warrant for arrest may block his access to safe shelter, subsidized housing, and benefits, so it may be best to surrender to the court in an effort to have it removed from his record. Our hope was that a charge from over a decade ago would be dropped due to Sidney voluntarily turning himself in to the court and his history of honorable military service.

Sidney was despondent at first, before eventually allowing me to both accompany him to court and advocate with the attorney and judge to dismiss the case. We not only stressed Sidney's Veteran Status and active-duty history of defending our country, but also spoke to his advanced age, level of disability (via medical and mental health note from Health Care for the Homeless), and that he had spent the last ten years in a "living hell" at The Night Center feeling alone and hopeless. During the courtroom proceeding, Sidney stood by my side noticeably trembling. He clutched my arm to balance himself and I assured him that we had made a convincing appeal for justice. The judge then announced that the local prosecutor had agreed to dismiss all charges. For the first time, I witnessed Sidney's smile and we left the courthouse with renewed hope.

---

[9] Heidegger writes about the concept that each communication, word, sentence, or phrase is composed of both the "said and unsaid" in his book *On the Way to Language* (1971). So, while the words are obvious to the listener or reader, the actual meaning is contextually based on the author's (sender's) culture, life experience, intent, and meaning, etc. To truly understand what is being communicated, the receiver needs to understand the greater context to what's been said, or in other words, cue into the "unsaid."

It took a great deal of courage for Sidney to stand up in court and face the consequences from an authority that he undoubtedly had little reason to trust. We felt thankful for the positive legal resolution. Sidney needed help, not punishment, as he had already suffered the negative impact of prolonged homelessness and loss. With the doorway to prison firmly closed, new opportunities awaited.

Sidney and I moved forward with applications for VA healthcare and financial benefits. As it turned out, he decided to stay at The Night Center while awaiting placement at the regional Soldier's Home. The Soldier's Home would provide Sydney with comprehensive services ranging from case management and healthcare to meals and transportation to all outside appointments. Approximately three months later, Sidney was approved for financial benefits and was accepted to the Soldier's Home. I carefully assisted with his transition to a new community environment. Sidney and I jointly reviewed with Soldier Home staff his homeless history and recent accomplishments, as well as his current challenges, needs and wants. In this manner, we shared with Soldier Home staff the Common Language that Sidney and I jointly created. Finally, after ten years of homelessness, isolation, and hopelessness, Sidney's "living hell," had come to an end.

Pretreatment Pathways

We all live, work, and play from within our "Houses of Language," which reflects our culture, community, our individual needs, wants, challenges, and past experiences of trauma and triumphs, as well as adaptations to the many environments in which we function. In this manner, the language we speak is unique, yet has much in common with others who have similar yet different sets of experiences that make up their world. In many ways, the language we speak and the context from which it has arisen impacts our perceptions and thereby colors our experience and further defines our worlds (Berger & Luckman, 1966; Freedman & Combs, 1996).

It is on the "Playground of Language" located between our Houses that holds the promise for constructing a Common Language that brings us together across cultural divides with the potential of creating meaningful dialogue that can lead to positive change. Being open to meeting people where they are at, engaging well, listening, and trying to understand their words, ideas and values is where it all begins. This is how our communities can be expanded, enriched and more inclusive of diverse perspectives that can better inform the realities that we construct.

Sidney's narrative, his interactions with the Outreach Counselor and the referral process that unfolded with other helping agencies and programs speaks to these challenges. Here, Sidney went from being isolated in a very harsh homeless environment of the streets and Night Center to community placement via the Soldier's Home, along with receiving needed VA (Veterans Administration) financial benefits and Healthcare services. This outcome was unimaginable to him at the start of our engagement, yet it became a possibility that we constructed through our interactions on the "Playground of Language." Our development of a Common Language allowed Sidney to hope for something better, and thereby form agreed upon goals (Contract) to guide our work.

Depending upon the client's needs and wants, we may make referrals and support the transition process to the many different houses of language among community resources. Beyond VA services and the Soldier's Home, referrals include a variety of programs ranging from Mental Health Clinics to self-help groups such as AA (Alcoholics Anonymous) or other Peer Support networks. For example, the house of language of a mental health clinic incorporates terms like "psychotherapy," "psychiatry," "psychotropic medications," "diagnosis," and so on. The intake process itself begins with the presumption that the client recognizes the need for help with a "mental illness," and will explore past "treatment" history and ask questions concerning past "psych hospitalizations," "suicidal ideation," etc. Similarly, the house of language of AA includes the twelve traditions and twelve steps, the concept of "surrendering to a higher power," and certain slogans like "One day at a time" and "Easy does it," among others. When one considers the cultural divides that may persist between the people we serve and these different referral options, it becomes quite evident that we need to build bridges between different houses of language to support the transition process.

In fact, the third stage of Common Language Construction (see Table 3, p. 59 - *Stage 3: Bridge Language*) is to support transition through a shared language. I call this bridging language. It is the process of discovering common terms and values that are a match between the interests, culture, needs and wants of the folks we serve with the mission, culture, and eligibility criteria of available resources and services inclusive of access to legal advocacy and representation. This means that it is necessary for the outreach counselor to be nimble in their interactions with the many different houses of language they are bound to encounter. Our work is often focused on reframing potential referrals and services through a Common Language that taps into the person's values and sense of meaning so it can be fully considered. We also do our best to prepare the intake person or initial contact for the arrival of the client by tapping into their house of language and sharing how our referral is consistent with their mission and eligibility criteria. Our goal is to prepare the referral source worker so they can provide a welcoming pathway paved by a common language. In this way, we are "translators" and "meaning makers" to build Pretreatment pathways to housing, treatment, and other resources. The following narrative further illustrates this process with the client, helping partners, and support services.

JoAnne's Story: A Spiritual Journey

While living and working in the Boston area, I received a phone call from a local Pastor. He was concerned about a woman named JoAnne who had been living by the side entrance of his church. The next day I went over to meet her. As I approached, I heard JoAnne singing a spiritual hymn in a loud and proud manner. She was a white female in her 50s parked right by the side entrance steps of the Church with an overloaded shopping cart covered by a tarp. She seemed well organized and reportedly at peace with her situation, despite living outside and having some evident swelling of her ankles. When I asked how she was doing, she responded, "With God's blessing, I am fine... Praise the Lord!"

This is how our first few interactions went. JoAnne would engage momentarily within the proximity of the church before stating, "God is watching over me so all is well." Realizing that I needed to begin with understanding her language, but not being religious myself I reflected her sentiments a bit hesitantly back by stating, "You are truly blessed!"

Over several meetings, I became more conversant in JoAnne's religious dialect and we formed a stronger bond. She continued to call me over to share a hymn and I always complimented her singing voice, while applauding her "spiritual" renditions. This inevitably brought a smile to JoAnne's face, while she bowed and showed gratitude for my time. JoAnne was delighted to have an audience for these short performances, and I understood that she valued sharing "God's word" with me. Yet I remained puzzled on how best to work together on a housing plan, as it was now late fall and winter was fast approaching. I knew that it was crucial to frame the offer through religious terms, so it could resonate and be actively considered.

At our next meeting, I asked JoAnne if she had thought much about the "advent" of winter and how hard it would be to stay outside. I further inquired about her health, and if her ankles and/or feet were bothering her. She stated, "Please don't worry about me. The Lord is my savior and I feel spiritually strong. If something bad was in the making, he would give me a sign." JoAnne then told me about her special relationship with the Pastor and that there were people within the religious community who provided her with shelter on cold nights. I now began to understand a little more on how JoAnne had adapted and found meaning in her current situation. She not only felt a deep spiritual connection with the church and Pastor, but also felt by God's directive protected by some members of the congregation.

My perception of JoAnne's circumstances was one of homelessness and high vulnerability. Yet JoAnne had a real sense of belonging and somehow managed to feel at home, while residing by the Church's side door entrance. Still, JoAnne's judgment appeared to be impaired by her religiosity, or preoccupation with religion, and she remained pre-contemplative of a variety of issues ranging from the condition of her feet and ankles to the need for a safe place to stay. This dual reality was my challenge to providing quality care. Was there a way to uphold JoAnne's deep connection to religion, spirituality, and the church, while simultaneously offering her needed resources and services?

This made me wonder if I could develop a Pretreatment pathway to healthcare and housing by engaging with the religious community. Maybe they could frame my offer in a way that could better resonate with JoAnne, through their shared sense of spirituality, caring, and purpose. I mentioned to JoAnne that I looked forward to meeting the

Pastor as he sounded like a very kind man who was spreading the word of love throughout the community. JoAnne nodded in agreement.

The following day, I contacted the Pastor to let him know that I had begun meeting with JoAnne. I was very interested to hear his take on JoAnne's situation and what he thought could be accomplished through my outreach. The Pastor had known JoAnne for many years as a devout and caring member of his congregation. He believed that JoAnne suffered from emotional difficulties due to an extensive history of domestic violence. He stated that after the passing of her abusive husband, JoAnne began staying right outside the church and proclaimed it to be her "haven from evil." He was quite clear about the need for JoAnne to reside inside, but felt very stuck.

In response, I explained the dilemma of JoAnne's inclination to wait for a spiritual sign before electing to move forward with any of the resources and services I could suggest. I then shared with the Pastor my knowledge of local housing resources inclusive of a Safe Haven program that specialized in serving women sleeping rough with a history of trauma or may have other mental health concerns. I further highlighted that this program was rent-free, provided nursing services right on site, and was within walking distance of the church. Without missing a beat, the Pastor exclaimed, "Our prayers have been answered... The Safe Haven program for Women is a godsend!"

I was very excited to hear the Pastor's endorsement of the Safe Haven program. Mirroring the Pastor's language, I stated that it would be very helpful to JoAnne if he could let her know that the Safe Haven option is an answer to our prayers. A godsend that she should seriously consider. The Pastor agreed!

As a result of my dialogue with the Pastor, a Pretreatment pathway to resources and services had now been developed. It was evident that words reflective of the Pastor's and JoAnne's language base included "safety," "godsend," and "prayers" and other religious terms. This helped me to frame palatable options for JoAnne to consider from our shared playground of language.

During the next round of outreach, I made an offering to JoAnne. We spoke about my recent communication with the Pastor and his enthusiasm about the local Safe Haven program. I framed the program as one that was designed to serve women and keep them "safe," while respecting their autonomy to participate in daytime and evening activities such as attending church services and other events. I also stated that it was quite "miraculous" that this type of rent-free housing recently got funded and currently had openings. JoAnne did not immediately respond, but appeared to be listening, as evidenced by her nodding her head and gently biting her lip. I then added, "The Pastor shared that it truly is a 'godsend' that will help many people." Fortunately, JoAnne was able to hear my offer, and uncharacteristically agreed to give it some consideration. I was encouraged when she shared her plan to check in with the Pastor later that day and hopeful that she had seen this as a "sign" to take meaningful action toward positive change.

With the Pastor on board, things quickly fell into place. JoAnne followed the recommendations of the Pastor and was now open to learning more about the Safe Haven program. With JoAnne's permission, we made arrangements with Safe Haven's staff for a tour and interview. I prepared the staff for JoAnne's arrival by sharing her dialect, religious convictions, and that she valued being a member of the church community. The staff understood the importance of welcoming JoAnne and orienting her to the Safe Haven, while upholding her spiritual-religious pursuits.

The staff began their tour with JoAnne by highlighting that folks were encouraged to engage in community activities of importance to them throughout the day. They then showed JoAnne a furnished bedroom with a comfortable-looking bed. On the door, we had placed a framed religious-spiritual poem—*Footprints in the Sand* (Author Unknown, 1978). When JoAnne saw this, she immediately felt at home. After approximately three months of doing outreach and meeting with the Pastor, JoAnne agreed to move into the Safe Haven's housing program.

Here, I supported transitions to a new environment by reframing the offer of the Safe Haven program within JoAnne's dialect for her due consideration, while simultaneously connecting with the expertise of the Pastor and preparing the Safe Haven staff for JoAnne's language base. The Safe Haven staff eagerly embraced the challenge and came up with the idea of placing the *Footprints in the Sand* poem on the bedroom door. By sharing JoAnne's religious-spiritual values with Safe Haven staff, we were able to create a psychologically informed environment

(PIE) to support JoAnne's transition to the residence. In the end, this was a group effort that only could have been accomplished through a common language that crossed cultural divides and thereby engaged all parties in our mission of finding JoAnne a home.

Meta-Language: Traversing Multiple Perspectives

Thus far we have reviewed Houses of Language of the person in need and the various systems of care and community settings they may encounter, such as Veteran services, MH Clinics, self-help groups—AA, Safe Haven Programs, religious communities, etc. Keep in mind that outreach counselors and their teams are also entrenched in their houses of language.

Outreach services are governed by their mission, values, and guiding philosophies. They espouse certain worldviews that are reflected through their daily work. Three common houses of language among outreach teams[10] are typically Clinical, Social Justice, and Religious/Spiritual.

A particular outreach philosophy or perspective dictates the types of questions asked, as well as the specific actions taken with those who are identified as needing assistance. On any given day, a person experiencing homelessness in an urban area may be contacted by different outreach teams who are working from varying perspectives. One can imagine the person who is unhoused sizing up the situation as the outreach worker approaches. They already know based on the individual or team coming their way what the script will entail. This ranges from whether they would like to pray together, focus on their rights, or access advocacy and/or legal counsel, or perhaps could benefit from mental health or detox services, etc. On a good day, housing options may be discussed or offered, but all too often housing resources are in limited supply or come with various eligibility requirements that may mirror the outreach team's sense of purpose such as mental health or substance use residential settings, or religious community-based placements, etc.

It is within this context that we can see the benefit of a Pretreatment approach. It is first and foremost focused on establishing person-centered

---

[10] This is not meant to be all-inclusive. Another prominent example is Peer Outreach workers from a needle exchange program practicing harm-reduction by handing out clean needles to intravenous drug users.

relationships and mutual goals that reflect the client's world. Rather than an outreach team's perspective dictating what options are offered, we uphold that people among the unhoused are experts in their own lives. Therefore, we respect their choice by providing a menu of housing possibilities and/or limited affordable residential options, as well as support services and other resources in response to the person's narrative, wants/needs and values. This aligns nicely with Housing First initiatives that uphold the person's autonomy to choose and their right to access a safe and affordable place to reside.

In this manner, Pretreatment promotes equity as it is based on grass-roots ecological social work of understanding people within the context of their environments, cultures, values, and aspirations. It speaks a humanistic language that goes beyond our own fear and pessimism to embrace one of hope and possibility. As interpreters and bridge builders, we perpetually advocate for greater access and connections throughout the community. We challenge the status quo of restrictive exact-match eligibility criteria and strive for a more inclusive best fit. More flexible and just criteria will serve more of those in need.

The value of Pretreatment is not just how it works on client and referral resources/services levels of care, but also in its function as a meta-language that promotes a greater perspective and communication across cultural divides that are often entrenched and may be at odds with one another. I have seen the power of this meta-language firsthand through my work with clinicians, medical care practitioners (e.g., Health Care for Homeless and Street Medicine staff), social justice advocates, religious leaders, and housing providers.

The core values reflected in Pretreatment's principles of care resonate well with these groups, among many others. People from these diverse fields share the basic tenets of our work as promoting safety, building trusting relationships and constructing a Common Language to establish effective communication. Likewise, getting goal-focused and supporting the process of transition and adaptation to new environments, resources and services, as well as facilitating positive change are not only non-controversial, they are embraced among providers, advocates, clinicians, medical practitioners, clergy, and others.

Clinicians and case managers will find that the language of Pretreatment also serves as a bridge between the worlds of Mental

Health and Addiction services. Rather than addiction counselors and mental health workers talking past one another, Pretreatment invites, creates, and promotes dialogue. This is because the integration of theory and practice that Pretreatment provides straddles both worlds. Stages of Engagement, Common Language Construction, and Supporting Transitions are grounding principles of Clinical Social Work practice and are central to quality mental health, Trauma and Psychologically Informed Care. Being goal-focused and working with people's strengths are derived from Psychiatric Rehabilitation and Solution Focused approaches. Likewise, Harm Reduction, Stages of Change, and Motivational Interviewing inform the Pretreatment perspective directly from the research base of addictions. In this manner, Pretreatment provides a meta-language that brings us together and effectively opens dialogue to better and more comprehensive care, rather than limiting us to the dualism, competing perspectives, and silos from mental health and addiction services.

Finally, Pretreatment provides an assessment language to guide staff within their service environments to discuss and problem-solve how best to intervene when our normal practices hit a wall, or are ineffective, or simply result in us wrongly asserting that the person we are attempting to assist is "not ready." An outreach perspective dictates that the person is always ready *if* we are willing to begin where the person is at.[11]

Pretreatment provides a guiding assessment language for our reflective practice based on an integration of its five principles of care with Solution Focus Model questions (Walter & Peller, 1992). For example, during 1:1 or group supervision or co-vision, we can examine how our work with clients is progressing along the Stages of Engagement (Pre-engagement, Engagement, Contracting). In addition to ascertaining what stage our work is in and thereby aligning ourselves and our interventions with the client, we can explore the following:

---

[11] It should be noted that some folks may not be a best fit for a particular service due to it not matching what the person needs or wants with what services can provide. This is distinct from the idea that someone is "not ready" to participate in the change process. An outreach perspective dictates that even when someone is in denial of their issues, there are effective ways to engage them and perhaps even begin the process of melting the pre-contemplative iceberg.

- What interventions have worked and what has not worked in the past toward promoting the engagement process?
- What interventions are currently working and what is not working in the present toward promoting the engagement process?
- What else can we add or try in the future to promote the engagement process?
- Have we jointly entered the contracting stage of engagement to establish a goal focus based on the person's needs, wants, and aspirations?

The same types of questions can be asked regarding Common Language Construction. This is also stage-based, so we would first determine what stage of language development we are working on (Understanding, Utilizing, Bridging Language), followed by these questions:

- What interventions have worked and what has not worked in the past toward promoting Common Language Construction?
- What interventions are currently working and what is not working in the present toward promoting Common Language Construction?
- What else can we add or try in the future to promote Common Language Construction?
- Do the goals we agreed to work on reflect the client's words, ideas, and values?

The above questions include asking ourselves more specifically what words, ideas, and values are welcomed and what is not welcomed on the client's playground of language.

- Are we using any words or terms that are currently triggering for the client, or have been in the past?
- Are there particular words, terms, ideas that we are currently using, or have used in the past, that have improved communication (spurring engaged conversations)?
- Are there any new words, terms, ideas that we can try in the future to improve communication?

We can continue our case exploration by considering our efforts toward Supporting Transitions, Promoting Safety, and Facilitating Positive Change. For each of these Pretreatment Principles of Care, we can ask Solution-Focus-based questions to promote reflective practice and productive staff dialogue about the fundamental challenges that they and their clients face.

Conclusion

Bakhtin states (1981, p. 342), "Language, for the individual consciousness, lies on the borderline between oneself and the other. The word in language is half someone else's."

In essence, we own only half of a word. Its meaning is ultimately shared between the sender and the receiver. This phenomenological truth teaches us to approach our work with great humility. Rather than us owning the process and dictating the terms of our interaction, it is a co-production. It is a dialogue between two people of different houses of language in search of a mutual understanding. Our hope is to find an agreed-upon guiding purpose defined by a common language that reflects people's world-experience, values, and aspirations.

A Pretreatment perspective provides us with the tools to facilitate productive dialogue across these cultural divides. It helps us and the people we serve to get unstuck and connected, thereby improving the quality of our lives, reducing feelings of helplessness, and staff burnout. Our mission is based on five guiding universal principles of care to promote greater inclusion of those in need. At its heart is the formation of person-centered relationships and a common language, while developing Pretreatment pathways to healthcare and other essential resources. Over the past two decades, the word of Pretreatment has spread, and so our mission continues throughout multiple fields of practice, which we will explore in the following chapters and beyond.

Table 3-1: Stages of Common Language Development[12]

Stages	Goals & Interventions
Understand Language	Attempt to understand a homeless person's world by learning the meaning of his or her gestures, words, values, and actions. Interventions include observing, listening, reflection, and asking what particular words and phrases mean, as well as learning what is important to the client.
Utilize Language	Promote understanding by developing and using a mutually agreeable set of terms. Build, modify, and use gestures, words, and phrases from the playground of common language based on the client's cues. Interventions include utilizing common language to ask client questions, explore the outreach worker's role, verbalize client's aspirations, and jointly define goals.
Bridge Language	Connect and integrate the common language developed between client and worker with other systems of language as defined by available services and resources (i.e., housing authorities, Social Security, medical services, mental health clinic, self-help groups, vocational programs, etc.). Interventions include connecting resources and services directly to client's goals, reframing commonly used words and phrases by targeted resources and services to be consistent with the playground of language developed by worker and client. Preparing for interviews via role play and accompanying the client may also be helpful. Prepare intake personnel of needed resources and services for the language that the client speaks. If certain phrases or terms may trigger a negative reaction, reframe and redefine these terms whenever possible, or seek accommodation.

Originally published: Levy, J. S. (2013). *Pretreatment Guide for Homeless Outreach and Housing First: Helping Couples, Youth, and Unaccompanied Adults*

[12] The process of Common Language Construction is based on ideas and concepts drawn from phenomenology and Narrative Psychology. Heidegger's book *On the Way to Language* (1971), and Epston & White's selected papers (1992), among others (Berger & Luckman, 1966; Freedman & Combs, 1996), which all influenced the formation of the above table.

References

Bakhtin, M.M. ([1935] 1981). *"Discourse in the novel," in The Dialogic Imagination: Four essays by M.M. Bakhtin.* ed M. Holquist, trans. C. Emerson and M. Holquist. Austin, Texas: University of Texas Press.

Berger, P., and Luckman, T. (1966). *The social construction of reality.* New York: Doubleday.

Derrida, J. (1976). *Of grammatology.* Trans. G.C. Spivak. Baltimore: The John Hopkins University Press

Epston, D. & White, M. (1992). *Experience, contradiction, narrative, and imagination: Selected papers of David Epston and Michael White, 1989-1991.* Adelaide, Australia: Dulwich Centre Publications

"Footprints in the Sand". *Church of God Evangel.* Vol. 68, no. 14. Cleveland, Tennessee. September 25, 1978. p. 27.

Freedman, J. & Combs, G. (1996). *Narrative therapy: The social construction of preferred realities.* New York: W. W. Norton Company, Inc.

Freire, P. (1970). *Pedagogy of the Oppressed.* New York: Seabury Press.

Heidegger, M., (1971). *On the way to language.* trans. Hertz, P. New York: Harper & Row

Levy, J.S. (2004). Pathway to a Common Language: A Homeless Outreach Perspective. Families in Society: *The Journal of Contemporary Human Services,* 85(3), 371-378.

Levy, J.S. (2010). *Homeless narratives & pretreatment pathways: From words to housing.* Ann Arbor, MI: Loving Healing Press.

Levy, J. S. (2013). *Pretreatment guide for homeless outreach & housing first: Helping couples, youth, and unaccompanied adults.* Ann Arbor, MI: Loving Healing Press.

Levy, J.S. with Johnson, R. (2018). *Cross-cultural dialogues on homelessness: From pretreatment strategies to psychological environments.* Ann Arbor, MI: Loving Healing Press.

NAACP Criminal Justice Fact Sheet (2023). https://naacp.org/resources/criminal-justice-fact-sheet

Walter, J. & Peller, J. (1992) *Becoming solution-focused in brief therapy*. Chicago: Brunner/Mazel.

4 A Career in Special Education through the Lens of Pretreatment

Virginia Bilz

> Tell me, I forget; show me, I remember; involve me, I understand.
>
> Xunzi—Ancient Chinese Proverb

Introduction

I wish I had known of Pretreatment twenty years earlier. When I graduated from college with a shiny new teaching license, I had visions of myself entering a brightly decorated classroom and spending the year smoothly guiding excited young minds through a combination of fascinating project-based learning and rigorous instruction. I would do this while maintaining a warm, nurturing approach that valued all my students as unique individuals. I was going to be great. Then I met my first class, eight young men residing in a juvenile treatment center with sentences ranging from six months (repeated car theft) to two years (aggravated assault and battery) to the heaviest hitter, a murderer midway through a seven-year sentence. I adjusted my vision and learned to rely upon the care workers and the social workers for help with tougher cases. I also learned to keep count of paperclips and every pair of scissors, but they were still students and I was their teacher. It worked but I made too many mistakes to ever believe myself to be great. Had I known then what I know now about the tenets of Pretreatment, outreach counseling and the stages of engagement, I believe I would have been a better teacher and a more effective agent for change in my students' lives.

I remained at that facility for nine years, but burnout was setting in and, eventually, I moved on to a special education teaching position at a medium-sized public school. It was a new population (there were girls in my classes!) and a lot more materials, but I no longer had the expertise of trained childcare workers and social workers on my team. I had my own classroom, but resources and support staff were stretched thin. As I got acquainted with my students, I began to see that special education students in the high school setting have often experienced some trauma at school, such as academic failure, isolation, bullying, and embarrassment at their identification as special education students. Some students may have had significant gaps in their education due to school avoidance, health concerns, or behavioral issues. Barely recognized in a small, homogenous community such as this is the bias that the family has already done the work to prepare the student for learning in school. However, this is just a convenient premise that is not always the case for students with disabilities. Often, for special education students, school has become a place of stress and struggle and, as with the people experiencing homelessness, asking for and accessing help becomes yet another task that seems beyond their abilities.

I was reminded of this when I read Jay Levy's book (2010), *Homeless Narratives and Pretreatment Pathways: From Words to Housing*. On a superficial level, the two populations, homeless adults and overwhelmingly housed, middle-class high school students, would seem to have little in common but, at the core, when viewed from the perspective of a teacher, there were important commonalities between the work Levy and his coworkers did and what I did every day as a special education teacher.

Later, when I read, *Pretreatment In Action: Interactive Exploration from Homelessness to Housing Stabilization* (Levy, 2021), I was again struck by similarities between the population he described and what I would call a core group of struggling special education students. Like those adults experiencing chronic homelessness, these students have often experienced years of failure due to external causes—being placed in classrooms without adequate supports due to undiagnosed or misdiagnosed learning differences or neurodiversity, family and homelife stressors, and/or economic disruptions, including unstable housing; or internal stressors such as brain-based difficulties or mental health challenges, including ADHD (Attention-Deficit Hyperactivity Disorder), Tourette's Syndrome, Bipolar Disorder and ODD (Oppositional Defiant Disorder). Again, in common with the chronically unhoused, these students are frustrated and distrustful and have frequently developed unproductive behaviors to protect their pride and their place within their social environment. Although the ultimate goal of my interactions with a student is academic success, not housing, that is seldom achieved without sorting through many of the challenges addressed in the Pretreatment Model.

In the Pre-Engagement Initial Phase, Levy describes identifying, approaching and communicating with an individual who may be eligible for and in need of services. Within special education, by the time I am working with a student, they have already been identified, evaluated, interviewed and, with the help of a team of educators, parents, psychologists and counselors, an IEP (Individualized Education Plan) has been written. This document outlines the help a student needs, carefully delineating services, times and location for each category of assistance. Problem solved and all is good, right? NO! Once this process has been completed, it's time for the real work to begin.

Relationship Formation

As with Levy's counselors and clients, services always begin with a meeting between the provider and the individual in need. As Levy (2021, p. 19) states, "Engagement is the foundation of our work." Although the student had been a participant in the entire evaluation process, they were usually unaware of what the next step would be and worried about how others would perceive them. A newly identified student's first visit to the special education classroom was often a confusing and embarrassing moment for them, especially if they were identified as needing services in their middle school or high school years. Whenever possible, I greeted a new student outside the classroom and away from the view of other students, introducing myself and describing what would happen within the room. I asked questions but did not press for answers, in the hope that I was presenting students with an opportunity to describe themselves but knowing that trust would need to be earned before they exposed any vulnerabilities. In the classroom, the student would see a wide range of "stuff and things" they might find interesting—books, small toys, humorous signs, items from nature, and even action figures. In trying to find a *common language* between myself and the student, I would talk about myself and my interests and listen in on conversations the student had with their peers. I paid close attention to clothing, stickers or patches they might wear, and ask generic sports or hobby questions that might reveal a personal interest.

Like Levy (2021, p. 23) approaching a reluctant client, I did "outreach in [a person's] general vicinity with clients who were more readily open to conversation." This would show the newer student that I could be helpful and that I could be trusted. When approaching the new member of the class, I did my best to sit across the table from them or ask to sit at the desk in front of them, always trying to give them a feeling of respect for their personal space. Once seated, I asked them if I could give them some help. For a few days or weeks, the answer was almost always "no," but I waited patiently for the time I would hear a "yes." If I was able to break through to the student on just one assignment, moving on to other assignments and other subjects usually followed. Sometimes a bond of trust wouldn't form between me and the student, but a spark would flare between them and another service provider within the room. This personal connection would finally open up the door to the ultimate delivery of needed help and services. It was a great moment when a student moved from resisting help and sullen silence to accepting assistance and, finally, to recognizing their need and asking for support. The following exemplifies this process with a student named "Ike."

Ike's Narrative

When I first met Ike, he was the picture of a "class clown." Often disruptive in classes, he worked hard to attribute his lack of academic success to both not caring about school and that, as a "sped," he abided by the credo (Saldanha, 2010), "better bad than stupid." Ike came into the Learning Support Program (LSP) classroom as a ninth grader, assuring me that he had no intention of doing anything. He sat at a desk away from others and refused offers of help from all the staff. He often engaged in distracting behaviors but, surprising to him, he didn't usually find others willing to join him.

The other students of the class, who were in 9th grade, were usually grouped around one paraprofessional who was helping them complete their science homework. The role of the paraprofessional is to build trusting relationships with the students, but unlike a teacher, not an evaluator, rather a nurturing center of support in LSP and academic classes. Every day, the paraprofessional, Carolyn, invited Ike to join the group but he stubbornly refused. He would slouch at his desk, staring at the table or working hard trying to engage other students in often silly behavior. As the days passed, Ike's grades, especially in science, began to reflect his attitude of non-engagement. Still, he resisted.

This continued for weeks until one day, towards the end of the first term, he casually sat down at Carolyn's table. There was no fanfare or mention of this change but, with the help of Carolyn and the group, Ike completed an assignment. Ike didn't say why he decided to join the study group, but I suspect the change was due to the relationship Carolyn had slowly built with Ike within the science classroom. Using gentle humor and a shared interest in motorsports, Carolyn had developed a common language and dialogue with Ike in that setting, which transferred over to the Learning Skills classroom. He had begun to feel a personal connection that allowed him to show some vulnerability within their relationship. A few days later, he completed another assignment. When the unit test arrived, Ike participated in the study session and came closer to passing that test than had happened before. Ike continued to be disruptive occasionally and would sometimes refuse to join a group, but he began to look for Carolyn when she was a little late to the LSP class. Ike and Carolyn had also developed a special handshake to celebrate his successes. As the year progressed, he passed one test and then another, ultimately passing the class. More importantly, Ike was able to extend this trust he had built to the other staff members and, the next year, was able to work with other staff and would even encourage incoming students to accept assistance.

Reflecting on Ike's turnaround through the lens of "Pretreatment," it is clear that Carolyn and Ike moved through the steps of the Pre-Engagement and Engagement process. Ike clearly had a need that Carolyn was able to identify: he was failing science due primarily to not completing assignments. Carolyn was able to offer a solution but, initially, Ike was not able to accept her help. Ike needed to see that other students were having success in an observably painless process. He watched and listened and sometimes tried to disrupt the process, but the group carried on. Each day, Carolyn engaged briefly with Ike and offered small bits of help in a common language that resonated in a non-judgmental manner, while always leaving a physical space (empty chair) for Ike to occupy if he chose to do so. There were no recriminations when Ike refused. When he did join, small successes were rewarded with praise, and other forms of help were offered. There were setbacks and outbursts on occasion but, overall, the goal of passing that science class was accomplished. By allowing Ike the time to adjust to the setting and by demonstrating what could be accomplished and what was needed from him, Ike was shown a pathway to access services and build the skills needed to promote a sense of achievement and independence.

Ecological Considerations: Supporting Transitions

In his book, *Pretreatment in Action,* Levy (2021, p. 57) suggests that in order to help someone, we must, "...observe strengths and challenges by understanding what works and what doesn't work through past and present attempts at transitions." Further, Levy identifies the importance of working with people's strengths and learning from their past experiences, as well as designing psychologically informed environments (PIE[13]) to facilitate positive change. Similar to human service case workers[14], my role as an educational liaison is to provide support, coordinate, and oversee the educational experiences of my students throughout their time at the school. In the classroom, I had many opportunities to learn about the strengths and challenges of my individual students and, sometimes, despite doing what they could to be successful, they still failed. In cases such as this, it was necessary to look at the system, identify the source of the challenges and to find different ways for the students to demonstrate their knowledge.

---

[13] Robin Johnson provides us with a detailed description of Psychologically Informed Environments (PIE) in the next chapter.

[14] Kate Shapiro shares her insights on the integration of case management services with a Pretreatment approach in chapter 6.

Georgi's Narrative

Georgi joined my Learning Skills classroom in his freshman year. He was a likable young man with abundant social skills, but he struggled with reading and written language production compounded by Attention Deficit/Hyperactivity Disorder. Georgi had been born in a Balkan country but was brought to the US as a child and was fluent in English. In his freshman year, getting Georgi to accept help had been a struggle. I knew his eighth-grade experience had been a disaster, with Georgi left feeling he was unable to be successful despite any attempts he made. His fellow students told me Georgi had reached a point in middle school where he simply refused to complete even the simplest assignments. Given this record of failure, he protected his ego by asserting that he didn't care about school, but staff could see that he was frustrated by the constant struggle.

By the middle of his freshman year, it was apparent that the team needed to review his Individualized Educational Plan. At this time, the team decided to change Georgi's schedule in order to transition him into smaller, more specialized classrooms for English and math. The slower pace and individualized attention with teachers who were able to build a trusting relationship with Georgi helped him turn his grades around. As he began to achieve some success, he became more invested in his work and was able to pass most of his classes, both regular education and special education. He was able to access help from teachers and paraprofessionals within his academic subjects and in the Learning Skills program. There were some setbacks but, overall, Georgi was experiencing success.

As Georgi's third year began, graduation looked closer and far more achievable, but he hit a roadblock a month into it. Perhaps because he was born in a foreign land to parents who grew up learning a different country's story, American history had always been a difficult subject for him. The subject material was based on a series of narratives that Georgi found hard to follow. When history grades were based on short assignments and frequent projects, with tests and quizzes asking for the recall of snippets of information, Georgi had a chance. His ability to memorize facts and being given the opportunity to demonstrate his knowledge through small projects had made it possible for him to pass his first American history class. US History II, however, was going to be much harder.

In the school system in which I taught, every teacher was free to present material and evaluate results in their own style. Some teachers stuck closely to a text, assigning daily or weekly readings and questions and using a standard/preprinted test provided by the publisher. Some teachers developed their own materials, seldom using a standard text and their tests reflected that approach, asking students to answer questions based on class discussions and notes. There were teachers who based a student's term grade primarily on daily or weekly work and others who put the emphasis on two or three lengthy exams each term.

This latter approach was the style of Georgi's junior year history class. Many students excelled in this class, as the teacher wove interesting facts about historical figures and places in the United States into fascinating lectures telling the story of the nation. Unfortunately, Georgi, with his limited attention span, was more likely to be looking out the window than listening and more interested in distracting his neighbor than hearing about the Gilded Age. When it came time to study for the test, the notes he had been given (because his notes were so sparse) made little sense to him without much memory of the accompanying lecture. When it came time to study and he looked at that sea of words swimming in front of him, once again everything and everyone surrounding him became so much more compelling than what was on those pages. When it came time to take the test, it was all long-answer essays, asking him to describe various governmental actions in detail, with no accompanying clues. Georgi was lost and he failed badly.

Realizing that these two styles—teacher instruction and student learning—were never going to be a good match, I discussed with the teacher that changing the test could be a solution. As Levy (2021, p. 67) says in his text, "Each person's journey of transition and adaptation is unique, yet it is up to the outreach counselor to find the best ways to support it." If I could create a manageable test and devise ways to help Georgi study for it, he might be successful. I began by carving out time from my other duties and after school hours. Using the lecture notes taken by a classroom paraprofessional, I created a test with a number of multiple-choice items and short answer questions (with a word bank) that identified the most essential people, places and ideas. I then crafted two longer questions that would address, in some form, the fundamental learning goals of the chapter. In this way, Georgi would be faced with a test for which he could effectively study and that still mostly addressed the learning objectives of the chapter.

To prepare for the test, Georgi was given a study guide tailored to the test (no extraneous information) and a set of flashcards that broke that chapter's information into small, easily absorbed bits of information. The flashcards were both online and on paper. Staff in Georgi's support class were able to repeatedly go through the flashcards with him and engage him in conversations regarding the two longer questions. The one-on-one conversations made it easier for Georgi to stay focused while also giving staff the opportunity to explain details and unfamiliar vocabulary.

When facing the first study session, Georgi complained loudly, fooling around and refusing to look at the flashcards. It was clear that Georgi did not believe there was any way he was going to pass that chapter test. If he invested time in studying and still failed, his pride would take a serious hit. If he could claim indifference and obviously hadn't studied, then the failure still left open the option to believe he would have passed if he had tried. Breaking through this self-imposed barrier was difficult, but staff persisted by cajoling, threatening and occasionally bribing (with candy) Georgi to study the flashcards and talk about the two essential questions.

Georgi took the test and he passed—just barely, but he passed! When the next test came around, he engaged more willingly in the study sessions and, again, passed. It may not sound like much, but Georgi's high-five was a pretty loud thank you. By the third quarter, when an upcoming test was mentioned in class, Georgi took to demanding to know when his flashcards would be ready and was regularly scoring in the 80s on the exams. Staff leveraged this impatience to get Georgi to participate in making the flashcards. He had cracked the code, knew how to be successful and was able to accept assistance. It was finally safe to show he cared about his grade.

Reflecting on my experience with Georgi, it was easy to see how he had been worn down by continual failure. Georgi had developed a multitude of unproductive coping strategies including disrupting the learning environment, disregarding or losing notes that were given to him, failing to complete assignments and refusing opportunities for assistance. At a critical transition point, we provided a psychologically informed environment (PIE) to facilitate positive change. He was given a great deal of 1:1 support and tutoring in a manner he could accept. This included the needed tools (focused study guide and flashcards) and an achievable goal (redesigned test he could pass) to be successful. This resulted in him risking his pride to study for a test with no guarantee of passing. He successfully overcame his sense of helplessness (stuckness), learned new information and passed several tests. Ultimately, Georgi had gained a sense of mastery in the classroom and felt pride in his accomplishments.

Facilitating Change: The Art of Enhancing Motivation

As many parents and most teachers know, in any battle of wills between an adolescent and one or more adults, either and/or both sides can take stubbornness and anger to very high levels. Bad decisions and regrettable choices can result, usually leaving everyone looking, in hindsight, for a better way forward. Unfortunately, often the holes both sides have dug themselves into in the heat of the moment are too deep to escape on their own and outside help may be needed. In a battle between parents and students, sometimes this help comes from the school, especially teachers, counselors and administrators who have built a relationship with the youth, away from the now contentious home environment.

Levy (2010; 2021, p. 89) frequently discusses autonomy and respect with regard to his clients, describing how goals need to be, "based on their [the client's] world and what they value in order to promote a sense of ownership and initiative towards reaching one's goals." Many times, in parent-adolescent conflict, the youth is asking for a degree of respect for their choices and a level of autonomy that a parent is not willing to accept or grant. Generally, this is a practical approach because most teenagers are not ready to make their own rules and cannot set healthy limits without some adult guidance and protection. It's why the juvenile justice system exists, and juvenile records can be sealed. Kids often make some very bad choices and it's up to the caring adults in their lives to lead them into better choices and help support the goals that have been set. Sometimes, though, the goals of the adolescent and the goals of the parents are not aligned. The parent may have a vision of the future of their child that doesn't match the youth's interests, skills or beliefs and the youth may have their own version of a future that the parents find frightening or impractical. Sometimes there is some middle ground and the two sides can agree on a compromise, sometimes one side capitulates and the two sides find a way to make it work but, other times, it all blows up.

Sara's Narrative

I met Sara when she was in 8th grade at her transition meeting. Every special education student facing a change of setting has a transition meeting near the end of the year to decide on how best to serve that student's needs in the new building. For the change from middle school to high school, the meeting is attended by the current middle school teachers, a special education teacher from the high school, the parents/guardians and hopefully the student. During the course of the meeting, the participants review the student's current progress, discuss student interests and goals, review course offerings, and decide on classes, settings (small group or large group) and the services the student will receive during their freshman year. If necessary, changes are made to the IEP (Individualized Educational Plan) to align the document to the strengths and needs of the student when they enter the high school setting. It is usually a quick and pleasant conversation, with the student and their parents looking forward to the exciting experience of moving on to high school. However, this was definitely not the case with Sara's meeting.

Sara was a lovely, perfectly groomed young woman of fourteen. It was obvious that she gave both thought and great care to her appearance, from her long blond hair and cosmetic use to her stylish, well-fitting clothing. It was not too surprising then when Sara declared her desire to be a cosmetologist and to attend the regional vocational school. Academic success had always been a struggle for her and, given her profound reading and writing disabilities, academic schoolwork was a long, hard daily slog.

Sara's parents saw the situation differently. Sara was intelligent (her neuropsychological testing had certainly shown that to be true) and if the school would work harder at meeting her needs, she could graduate from the academic high school and go on to college. Sara's father, a first generation Portuguese-American and hard-driving lawyer, would not consider the idea of her attending a vocational school, insisting that she next attend the local high school and he would make sure the school did everything necessary in order for Sara to achieve academic success. College was absolutely the goal. Sara protested that she was not interested in college, crying and arguing that she knew what she wanted and the vocational high school was her choice. Sara's mother stayed passive during the discussion and, in the end, the decision was made that Sara would attend the local academic high school and the group would write an IEP that identified this setting and the supports she would need there. Case closed.

I became both Sara's English teacher and her educational liaison. The purpose of the liaison was to be just that—a liaison or bridge between the parents and the special education central administration and the regular education teachers, the idea being that I would try to solve problems before the parents or teachers felt the need to move the issue up to the administrative level. Over the next two years, I fielded a number of emails and calls from Sara's father demanding to know why certain things weren't being done in accordance with the IEP and his frequent criticism of both the education and grades Sara was receiving. I would investigate his complaints and then do my best to explain how certain situations had played out. Often, it was a matter of assignments that had not been completed and Sara telling the story in a manner that blamed the teacher, not her. Sometimes Sara's father was correct, and Sara's IEP was not being followed in an appropriate way. In that case, it was necessary for me to somehow find time to meet with the regular education teacher and suggest ways to help them meet their obligations towards Sara and her learning needs.

During those first two years, I came to know Sara well. I knew her father traveled frequently for work and the times he was home were marked by an imposition of rules and demands that Sara found much too constricting. Her mother tried to keep a semblance of peace between the two strong personalities, siding with Sara when the father was away but taking the father's side when he returned. Sara became adept at playing this situation to her advantage but, as her teacher for two periods a day, I could see her anxiety building. She spoke often of her parents arguing and the tense atmosphere at home.

As time went on, Sara grew steadily more angry and resistant. Toward the end of her sophomore year, Sara's friend group started to change and she began socializing with older students. These new friends gave her rides to school and she often arrived late. She was suspended for five days for using marijuana in school and at the meeting held during this suspension, she was unrepentant and defiant. At the beginning of her junior year, in the middle of all of these changes, on a particularly emotional day for Sara, she told me that her parents had split up and her father had moved out of the house. Despite all the arguments she had witnessed, Sara was infuriated that her father had deserted her mother. She felt betrayed and hurt, taking her mother's side, and was vocal in her disgust at her father's behavior. Her mother was devastated and Sara's home life was in turmoil.

With only her devastated mother trying to impose daily discipline, Sara began pushing rules and restrictions beyond acceptable limits. Sometimes, she stayed out all night and became involved with a young man who had left school and was living in an apartment with another former student. Both young men were known to be a bad influence (suspected drug use, among other things), so Sara's former friends began to steer clear of her and her new social circle. Sara's attendance at school became sporadic and her parents came together to issue an ultimatum: end the relationship and follow the rules of the house or leave. To no one's surprise, Sara left and moved in permanently with her boyfriend.

Despite this drastic change, Sara continued to attend school. She wanted to finish high school but was struggling to do so. I had started this journey with Sara in 8th grade and was determined to see it through to the end. The school administration and her parents called a special education meeting to discuss this new situation and we convened with many questions and a frantic hope for a resolution. Importantly, I insisted that Sara attend because this meeting was all about her and the group needed to hear her words. She was the only one who could truly express her needs and goals. Sara clearly articulated to me that she needed to be heard and this gave her that opportunity. In this manner, I believe that Sara knew she wasn't alone. I was there for her and attended the meeting.

The meeting had a contentious beginning. There was anger between the newly divorced parents, frustration with Sara's flaunting of the rules of both school and home, and Sara's feelings of disempowerment in the decisions that were being discussed. As liaison, I tried to give everyone a chance to be heard and slowly a path forward began to emerge.

Everyone at the meeting had a stake in the results. Sara wanted her freedom and she still talked of becoming a cosmetologist. Sara's mother wanted Sara to be happy, safe and freed from the father's demands. She had come to accept this future career for her daughter. By now, Sara's graduation from high school was paramount to her father. Regular attendance and adherence to school rules were the goal of the administration. The improvement of Sara's academic skills was the goal of the special education department.

In the end, a plan was developed that could meet the basic requirements of all stakeholders if everyone was willing to bend and to accept certain facts of this new situation. Sara was out of the house and she had no plans to return, but she did see the importance of her high school diploma. On the school front, in her favor was the fact that she had consistently passed all of her classes in her freshman and sophomore years and so had the cushion of a few extra credits built up going into her junior year. She was currently keeping her head above water in her eleventh-grade English, math and history classes and passing those three classes for the year would give her enough credits to become a senior the next year. On the life-skills front, now freed from her husband's insistence on college for Sara, Mom had been quietly exploring the possibility of Sara working at a friend's salon. The friend knew Sara well and thought she could be a help as long as she was reliable.

Sara declared she wanted to attend high school, but she was extremely anxious about being "trapped in the building" for the full schedule of seven classes per day. Could she go to school for only the required periods? The administration was resistant but ultimately agreed to allow Sara to attend for only three periods every day. To make her three classes consecutive, the guidance office would change Sara's English class to one that met a period adjacent to her history class. Unfortunately, the single special education Algebra II class could not fit into the desired schedule, so I agreed to be Sara's Algebra II teacher during an LSP class. Although I wasn't certified as a math teacher, I had co-taught an Algebra II class for two years and knew the material.

The housing arrangement, Sara living in an apartment with no restrictions and excessive "partying," was one that made none of the adults happy. Sara insisted she was safe, that her boyfriend treated her well and encouraged her to stay in school. It was no one's first or even second choice but the feeling was "that ship had sailed." Sara was not coming home.

The only legal recourse would mean the involvement of the Department of Children and Families and perhaps the filing of a CHINS (Child In Need of Services), and with Sara being seventeen years old, there was little the state could or would do. The hope now was to keep lines of communication open in the belief that Sara might decide on her own that home would be a more comfortable option.

The new schedule was created and Sara agreed to a contract with the principal that stated she would be on time to school, would miss no more than three days of school over the next two terms, would leave the building when her three classes were over and would not bring drugs onto the premises. She consented to random searches of her handbag. Sara was set up with an internship at the local salon with her mother's friend for four days a week and would receive school credit for the experience. Sara's father agreed to continue to pay Sara's car insurance and upkeep so Sara would have a reliable form of transportation. For her part, Sara agreed to communicate daily with her mother and complete her assignments. The guidance department agreed to be available to Sara if she felt overwhelmed and the plan was put in place, to begin the following Monday.

To almost everyone's surprise, the plan was a success. Sara attended school faithfully and completed most of her assignments—many more than she had done in the past two terms. Her supervisor at the salon was very happy with her work ethic and agreed that Sara had great instincts with regards to cosmetology and hair styling. Sara was on time to school and participated in her classes. She kept in touch with her mother and to everyone's relief, when she broke up with her boyfriend that summer, she moved back into her mother's house.

Sara returned to school in the fall for her senior year and graduated on time, with her class, participating in the multitude of senior activities and walking across the stage to receive her diploma. The following fall, she enrolled in cosmetology school.

Looking back on Sara's situation through the lens of the Pretreatment philosophy, it sheds light on how the situation escalated and ultimately spiraled out of control. At that meeting in eighth grade, the adults in the room had asked Sara to identify her goal and when she did, this goal was ignored. Not very many fourteen-year-olds have a firm vision of their future but Sara did. As Levy states (2021, p. 39), "The greater our understanding of people within the context of their narratives, the more we can work with, rather than inadvertently working against their values, aspirations, and sense of meaning."

As Sara made her way through high school, she continued to chafe against the academic demands made on her. Although she could understand a lecture, draw sophisticated conclusions and ask good questions, her efforts to complete the basic tasks of reading and writing were always a struggle. There were ways to alleviate many of her difficulties, such as listening to recorded books instead of reading, and using word-predictive software, grammar check, and speech-to-text software when writing, but all of these techniques left Sara feeling different from her friends. She wanted no part of any of them. To her, all this effort was just a continuation of her ongoing stress. She was experiencing, in Levy's words (2021, p. 90), a sense of "stuckness," in which the school and her parents were asking her to keep trying despite the stress of a lot of difficult efforts that seldom resulted in real success. She knew where her greatest strengths lay and it wasn't in the written word.

As her home life became increasingly chaotic, Sara began to act out more in school and at home. Through all this, though, she was able to hold on to her desire to get her diploma. She continued to trust her teachers and counselors in the high school, reaching out and responding to the many efforts to keep her invested. Although she was very angry with her parents, she maintained contact. She came to that final meeting and held her own through the hard discussions. When she was able to see an achievable goal and feel included in the plan that was in line with her values and aspirations, she bought into it. As Levy states (2021, p. 91), it is better to, "join with the person on their quest for change, rather than allowing people to feel alone, isolated, overwhelmed, and powerless."

Conclusion

In my thirty years as a special education teacher, I have taught young people with a wide range of abilities and limitations. Some students were a joy, some were a challenge, while most fell somewhere in between. I could wish for schools to see what I came to value in Pretreatment as a better way to support students and reduce educator burnout. Pretreatment provides universal principles of care to help guide our work. How I wish this was put into good use within the school context, thereby providing the space for group learning and problem-solving to facilitate better outcomes for our students. Levy (2021, p. 113) states, "In essence, we are building trusting relationships that respect our workers' autonomy, while demarcating the time and space in our schedules to foster a sense of team, reflective practice and a culture of Enquiry." I often think of how much more effective I and the paras in the LSP room could have been had reflective practice, with the time and space to meet, had been a regular part of how the school functioned.

When I read Jay Levy's books, I saw that there was a thread that ran through Levy's approach to his clients that matched my experience with my students. For me, like Jay Levy and his counselors, success rarely came without a trusting relationship between a facilitator and a person in need. There were usually barriers to the formation of this bond of trust, some internal, some external but persistence, caring and creativity could lead to a positive result. There were often setbacks or reversals. In Levy's case, perhaps a healthcare, housing, or legal issue for the client; in my case, a new classroom setting that was a poor academic fit or a change in the student's living situation, but the more ownership and involvement the individual could feel in the process of resolution, the more likely a solution would work. Like the caseworkers on the street, I have experienced frustrations—with students, parents, colleagues, school administration, the entire educational system, but I have also experienced the satisfaction of knowing I have helped someone reach a goal and move to a new dimension in their life. And that feels pretty damn good.

References

Hutton, E. L. (2014). An Exhortation to Learning. In *Xunzi: The Complete Text* (pp. 1–15). Princeton University Press. https://doi.org/10.2307/j.ctt6wq19b.6

Levy, J. S. (2010). *Homeless narratives & pretreatment pathways: From words to housing*. Ann Arbor, MI: Loving Healing Press.

Levy, J.S. (2021). *Pretreatment in action: Interactive exploration of homelessness to housing stabilization*. Ann Arbor, MI: Loving Healing Press.

Saldanha, K. (2010). *It's better to be bad than stupid: An exploratory study on resistance and denial of special education discourses in the narratives of street youth*. Doctoral Dissertation, University of Toronto, Canada.

Ancient Chinese Proverb: The quote comes from Xun Kuang (Chinese Confucian philosopher who lived from 312-230 BC) in the book *Xunzi*.

5 Pretreatment: PIEs in the Micro-Social World

Robin Johnson

> If you want to go fast, go alone. If you want to go far, go together.
>
> African Proverb

A Meeting of Minds

When I came across Jay Levy's writings on Pretreatment all the way back in 2014, my first thought was: here is a kindred spirit.

It was not just the intelligent compassion in his deeply respectful, person-centred approach. Nor was it just his evident commitment to thinking through, analysing and sharing his ideas on "what works:" to spell out with just a few key themes where the essential ingredients are in these interactions. This kind of analysis had a lot in common with the approach I had been taking myself, in writing about what works in providing services for this same group. That was one clear thing in common.

Certainly, there was a clear difference between our worlds and our work. His focus at that point was primarily on homelessness outreach and assessment, supporting the transition through to permanent housing, working in the spirit of the Housing First approach. My own work, at least until then, had been primarily in accommodation-based support services, and all the stages of resettlement that the Housing First programme had wanted largely to skip over.

Jay's work on Pretreatment is already expanding beyond the realm of homelessness outreach and assessment, and finding validity in many other areas where we must engage people first and foremost on their own terms. Likewise, in this essay I will be showing the ways in which the PIEs concept has spread far beyond its original roots in the UK's homelessness "hostels."

For the US reader, let me first explain that "hostel" here does not mean a youth or travel hostel. This is the term we use for what you in the US now call "interim housing." The UK has made great efforts over some thirty years to improve the quality of our hostels. My work on "psychologically informed environments" (PIEs), which reflected my many years working in community mental health and later a scant few as a government adviser, researcher and journal editor, was all a part of that development.

We were also writing in and for different contexts. There were evident differences between the US and the UK: different geography and scale, different institutions, and some different technical terminology for programmes and services. This last, it became clear, is at the root of a lot of miscommunication and the many wasted opportunities to learn from each other. He and I later made this a central issue in a book we then co-edited: *Cross Cultural Dialogues on Homelessness: From Pretreatment Strategies to Psychologically Informed Environments*.

Still, there was something to this Pretreatment approach that clearly echoed our work. These conversations with Jay matched and complemented many other discussions I was having here in the United Kingdom with workers from a host of other services who were, it seems, finding the ideas I had been putting forward equally relevant to their own work.

In fact, it would be fair to say that the many conversations I then had with Jay, whether in writing, by phone, video, or in person, played no small part in the shift in my own thinking and approach over these past few years.

These conversations all helped to extend the original, more hostels-based PIEs model to cover this far wider range of responses to the challenges of homelessness. In outreach services, in street engagement, in our own (then fairly new) Housing First projects, and in a string of other contacts beyond those we had originally had in mind, there was something here that needed bringing out. Still, it took some while to tease out just where this common ground lies.

At a conference in 2017 on the research and evidence on PIEs, I had therefore proposed a working party to consider updating the original versions of the PIE. Along with, for example, Housing First, Trauma Informed Care, the strengths model, recovery and a number of other similar developments, I had included Pretreatment in the list of new issues to be encompassed, even though at this time Pretreatment was almost completely unknown this side of the pond.

What, then, is this common ground, that I was keen to explore?

Common Ground

In a chapter in the *Dialogues* book (Levy & Johnson, 2018), I had suggested that Jay's work helped to pinpoint what I came to call the core skills in engagement, those that are needed in any setting, whether in 1-1 work, in street outreach, or in any advice centre, day centre, shelter, or in ongoing support to individuals in their own homes. In all the steps on the pathway to settled accommodation, I suggest, these skills will be in play.

In fact, these skills are essential even in explicitly therapeutic work. Without that original engagement, no other techniques can get traction. If in the past they have barely been mentioned in the literature of therapy, I suspect this is simply because in explicit therapy, the "client" is already primed and usually motivated to engage. That primary Pretreatment work had been done, by the client, and now is taken for granted.

If these are the underlying skills, what my own work had done was to look at the wider context in which these individual interactions occur, and how to think through and design these contexts—how to see them as environments that may support or inhibit these interactions, and how to develop the possibilities to be constructive.

We had originally said that any service "that takes into account the psychological make-up—the thinking, emotions, personalities and past experience—of its participants in the way it operates" could be described as a psychologically informed service (PIElink[a], n.d.). But these days we have tended to reserve the term for those that did so consciously, for a purpose; and many are doing so with the aim of creating a service "in the round," as we say in the UK (meaning "seen from all angles, perspectives or aspects," or "treated thoroughly with all aspects shown or considered").

Then we have what we can properly call a psychologically informed environment. In short, many psychologically informed services are providing some of the key ingredients, but it's the PIE that is the whole package. Although if that makes it all sound like something new, more work to do on top of what you already do, what we find is that for many, perhaps most services, it isn't. It's just a way to see the whole thing more clearly—to see it "in the round" (Johnson, 2023a).

Even so, the actual "environments" in services that we'd had in mind in those first few years had been buildings. We talked of "the built environment and its social spaces," arguing that this must be seen as one of the key components, and not a mere context and an afterthought. In services and buildings that we manage, we can have some control over the design of the building: reception areas, lighting and signage, reserved access areas. We can then, with sufficient awareness, start to develop and design these spaces to best suit the purpose of engagement, the better to meet clients' needs.

But how, then, can we use that same awareness of the significance and potential use of these spaces for more engaging interactions in environments that we do not own, and cannot control?

Jay's writings had given us some pointers, and these and many other conversations with others then started us off on the trail. It took a while, but I eventually began to see that the key to this was to look at what these spaces mean not to us, but to the other person. These are, after all, the spaces they live in; or those that we hope they will want to.

Incidentally, although we do talk of using "psychology" in a PIE, this is not restricted to the insights that clinical psychologists, psychotherapists and others may bring to the party, useful though they may often be. Nor is it the psychology of academic and research studies that see the experience of individuals from the outside, looking in. Instead, we are referring to our attempts to grasp the world as it is experienced, the world-as-it-is-to-them.

This is what ethologists, those who study wild animals in their natural habitat, have called their "Umwelt" (Kull, 2001; Yong, n.d; Cummings, n.d). This goes both wider and deeper than anything therapists will see in their clinics; and it gets to the heart of the common ground between all constructive interventions. (PIElink[b], n.d.)

Let's look at a few examples.

Spaces as Opportunities

When we approach and enter someone else's personal space, it is important to understand what that space, and the choice of that space, may mean to them. Whether it is a piece of cardboard in a doorway, a tent in the woods, a railway arch, we must start with the assumption that the individual has made their own choice of that space, for reasons with a meaning to them that we must try to appreciate. We will need to show some appreciation and respect for the boundaries we may cross, or be invited to cross. Entering someone's space is a deeply personal action.

There are researchers who have studied the implied messages in physical proximity. The anthropologist, Edward T. Hall, suggested some years ago used the term "proxemics" for the study of the meanings of personal space, and how people relate to and negotiate these zones with an implicit understanding. (This is best shown visually, so it's worth looking up some of the videos you will find on the internet. The links at the close of this chapter will take you to a few, to get you started.) (PIElink [c], n.d.)

Here I am also reminded of a conversation with a nurse in a drop-in centre near one of Paris' major railways stations, "where the ragged people go," as Paul Simon put it. As a nurse, she could change dressings, apply ointments. In her role, she had a licence to touch, permission for intimacy. "Sometimes," she said to me, "this may be the only time in days or weeks that they have felt a human touch" (PIElink [d], n.d.). That is just the sensitivity, the awareness that I wanted to recognise.

The same awareness of the importance of boundaries applies, even when they are codified into residency and tenancy rights. As we enter someone's personal space, in their own home—or even just a room in a hostel or a bedspace in a shelter—we can try to appreciate the personal meanings that people invest in that space. However small and insecure, it is populated, so to speak, and "informed" with the meanings of their own life.

Personalised Space

Some years ago, an occupational therapist, Leonie Boland, gave a presentation to the annual Pathways conference on a study she had conducted of working to help anchor and enrich the sense of being at home, in your own space at last, for people newly re-housed. Her project involved simply giving a number of residents a camera to take, and later to show, photographs of their homes, of what they had found and what they had done to make it a home (PIElink [d], n.d.).

All the "personalisation" here was their own doing, but it was the creative idea in the staff support team that had helped them to do it. There was no requirement to put into words what these photographs said about them, and the place, although it might often unlock a conversation. But just to value what they had done, by implication, was sufficient intervention to affirm and enhance this home-making—to bear witness, as Jay has put it.

For another example, there is a drop-in service for street homeless people in the heart of Glasgow, run by the Simon Community. Their approach, and in fact their whole building, had been completely remodelled after attending a seminar on the PIE approach. The new building is on the main street, and it is designed to be light and airy. It is a transformation from what people might expect of a homelessness centre.

For one thing, they did away with the reception desk. The layout of the reception area looks more like a café. As you enter, staff, or others in the centre, walk up to you. Some of the rooms upstairs are made available to other outreach services to use, to base some staff there. When an individual is ready to talk to someone, there is no labyrinthine referral process or lengthy wait to make an initial contact (PIElink [d], n.d.).

But there is one other tiny feature of that environment that speaks volumes. One member of the new staff team decided one day to bring into the open reception area a handful of potted plants. Everybody liked them, so they brought in some more. Soon the place was as green as a garden centre, and what they found was that some of the street homeless people coming there began to help out with the watering (Webster, n.d.).

It took on. Now, when one of their centre users does get a flat to move to, they get to take one of these plants with them. The plant sits there as a reminder of the help they have had, the care they have shown and been shown. Back at the centre, these plants all around are now tokens of optimism for a new future.

Open Spaces

This takes us to another of the innovations of PIEs 2: the appreciation and conscious use of local networks and surroundings as part of the service.

One hostel-based psychologist talks of going for a walk in the local park with one of the residents, a man with chronic schizophrenia who can be quite withdrawn and hard to reach, while at the hostel. But in the park, she was amazed to find how well he knew all the animals, especially the ducks, and how he would chat freely with the park staff. Give him a new environment to be in, and a whole new side to this man came out (PIElink [d], n.d.).

Another worker, in an outreach team, describes taking one of her caseload to an appointment in her car. What she found—and more to the point, what she noticed—was that the relationship changed. They spoke more freely as they travelled together. Where usually making eye contact is very valuable for creating a sense of relations, of value in the person, there are times when not sitting face to face can open up new territory, and it's far more practical and cheaper than the psychoanalyst's couch, that cliché so beloved of cartoonists (PIElink [d], n.d.).

Another service for young people has youngsters who, after a period in the hostel to stabilise and form relationships of trust with the support staff there, continue to get their support from the same hostel staff team, as they move out to a flat of their own. They see this as a clubhouse model, or a core-and-cluster.

Once they used to have follow-up keyworker sessions in the youngsters' new homes, or in the counselling room at the hostel. Now they are just as likely to have these sessions in a coffee bar. It's true that there is not the privacy of a dedicated counselling room; confidentiality is a little porous. But as they told me, talking about life and problems in a coffee bar is normalcy for young people (and for many others too). This is the life they are helping prepare their youngsters for (PIElink [d], n.d.).

Another service, working with highly vulnerable sex workers in the north of England, encouraged group discussions between the clients. One day, as it was hot, they decided to take the discussion out into the local park. For many, it was the first time they had used the park not to turn tricks, but as citizens, with as much right as anyone to be there. They were reclaiming the space, and the meaning of the space for them, a small but valuable step toward healing the internalised stigma in their lives (PIElink [d], n.d.).

Incidentally, not all constructive discussion groups need to be formally therapeutic. In a Bristol women's drop-in, also there to provide respite and a safe space off the streets for sex workers, the staff attempted at times having talking therapy groups. No-one came. When instead they established a regular session of knitting, it was immediately popular; and there the women talked freely about their lives, what stressed them, and how they coped. (PIElink [d], n.d.).

Shared Spaces

All together, these examples are a reminder that many valuable activities that are very positive for mental health, particularly in involvement in group and community activities, are not seen as "treatment." Sadly, the health benefits of participation in these were often only fully appreciated when described as therapy, for example, animal assisted therapy, eco-therapy.

But this last is also a reminder that although we speak here of personal space, not all uses of space are simply individual. We now know that isolation is as bad for health as smoking, and group and community support is especially helpful to those recovering from addictions, whether chemical or behavioural. Many accommodation placements have failed because the re-housed individual missed the community of the street, where they could be somebody.

For street drinkers on a park bench, the comfort of easy acceptance of each other among drinkers may be skin deep and collusive, but we ignore the importance of these social bonds at our peril. This, too, is a use of what we might call the "found environment" to meet deep psychological and personal needs for companionship, and we can learn to recognise and respect that.

Sector Engagement

More commonly, though, we find services working to encourage and facilitate engagement of their service users with other valuable support services and organisations outside their own service. In the PIEs 2 framework, we call this "sector engagement" because to give it a name, and a place in the framework, is to give this recognition and encouragement as a valuable and a potentially intrinsic part of the work.

One CEO of a small voluntary organisation working (again) with drug-using sex workers in inner London told how much of her initial work in creating their services was with the local police force, to explain what they were doing, to give them the space and time to work with these woman, and to get them to see their charity not as a nuisance but as a valuable resource to them (PIElink [d], n.d.).

Many social housing agencies in the UK will be active in attending events to discuss local needs, gaps and barriers, and exploring how to work through them with other agencies involved. Many are highly proactive in running events and training, not just for their own staff and service users, but for all agencies in their locality.

So, we can see how the PIE approach, as it has evolved over 10+ years, is now far wider than just the attention to these immediate services as environments, but must extend to the wider context in which these services themselves, for good or ill, are situated (PIElink [e]).

Using the Rest of the Framework

Even so, working with and helping to create these "spaces of opportunity," as we call them, is still just one of the five themes or clusters of practice elements in the full PIEs framework. We call them the "Big Five," taking that phrase from psychology, where there are said to be five key dimensions of personality.

The other four themes in the PIEs 2 framework are: working with and enhancing the "psychological awareness" embedded throughout the service, emphasising "staff training and support," developing an attitude of "learning and enquiry," and finally what we call "the Three Rs:" giving thought to the day-to-day running, the rules and the available roles for staff and for users that a service can offer, plus the overall responsiveness of the service, to make up the threesome.

This is not the time or place to go into all the possibilities here. We have, after all, an entire dedicated website through which to explore the full range of the approach (*ibid*, PIElink[a], n.d.). But here, we can tease out just a couple of issues, as further examples. Let's look a little closer at a couple of these PIEs 2 practice elements that relate to Jay Levy's own working practice, in the REACH team he managed in Western Massachusetts (PIElink [d], n.d.). These will then illustrate the ways the PIEs framework now connects with Jay's work as he has described it in several of his earlier books, and in many videos and radio interviews.

As we've said, the PIEs approach places great emphasis on training and support for the staff, in recognition of a growing understanding of how emotionally demanding this work can be. In one of Jay's earlier books (Levy, 2021, pp. 111-28), he focussed on this aspect of the PIEs framework, to stress the importance he places on supervision for his workers. Like Jay's work, the PIE approach also encourages reflective practice, both as a form of staff support—listening to their own thoughts on what they might learn—and so enhancing the responsiveness of the service. In fact, this is seen as one of the key pillars, sometimes described as the "golden road" to developing as a PIE.

Relationships: Continuity and Witness

But let's also mention another element not just on the thinking but on the practice in Jay Levy's own team's work in the REACH service that does particularly well reflect and exemplify one of the Three Rs in the PIE framework: the value in thinking through the range of roles on offer in a service.

Jay has written extensively about this in his earlier books (Levy, 2010, pp. 116-119; Levy, 2013, pp. 112-115). As he describes it, the workers who first made contact with a homeless individual—the outreach part of their work—will continue to work with that individual as they take the first steps towards temporary (or "interim") - housing; and a worker, connected through a common language, from the same team will continue to work and keep in contact, as they move on, to settled accommodation.

Rather than passing the individual over to a new set of workers and having to start over to establish the same level of trust and communication afresh, the continuity in these working relationships that the REACH service can provide is not just a practical arrangement. It shows a marked respect for the value of the relationship.

In one of the interviews I had with Jay, we discussed how the worker is then a witness to the progress the individual has made. As with Boland's study of photo-reportage, (PIElink [d], n.d.), this is affirmation as a form of support. It is comparable, clearly, to the clubhouse approach of the youth service I'd mentioned earlier. In both cases, and there are many more such examples, this ongoing relationship then offers a new dimension of stability, beyond the terms of the tenancy alone.

It is a sad fact that the way so many services are funded, with tightly focussed, outcome-specified and time-limited targets to reach, actually militates against realising the value of the relationships of trust, as pivotal to success. But we'll come back to that, in a page or two.

Where to Now?

The picture I have painted here so far is one of a new spirit in homelessness services, that we in the UK and Jay and his teams in the US have been exploring, each trying to identify the key features. It is one that has evolution and innovation at its heart. So these efforts are ongoing, and perhaps always will be. Jay's work evolves, just as ours does here in the UK, as this new book will show.

What next, then? Let us end this essay with trying to look ahead a little, because the PIE idea, it seems, is spreading, and in three main ways.

Extending Within and Throughout the Service

First, one of the major developments in some of the more recent PIE discussions—in the informal, online forums to which all PIElink community members are invited—has been the need for embedding the PIE approach throughout the whole of the agency, "from top to toe," and even beyond, into work with others partners and services in the locality (*ibid*, The PIElink[e], n.d)

As our understanding has grown of the importance of the environment as a context, and of tackling issues in the context, so the concept of working with the built environment and its social spaces has grown from just looking at the buildings we use, to considering the surroundings and networks, to the systems and pathways, opportunities and barriers.

We have already mentioned the work of many agencies in reaching out to other services in their locality, to understand better the needs and the barriers in their area. In the PIEs 2 framework, we call this "sector engagement" (PIElink[f], n.d). This kind of reaching out to understand includes also discussions with local commissioners and other funders, whose expectations of what services should do will form the context in which they and we must work—the business environments, so to speak.

Extending Outward, to Other Countries

Second, this idea may have begun with our observations of a radical shift in practice around the turn of this century, seen most clearly in homelessness and housing support services, at first, largely for historical reasons, mainly in the UK. But the idea is being taken up by services and governments also in Europe. Australia is closely following.

The US and Canada may well be next. Certainly, there is a significant recent reframe in US federal government policy and funding, that now sees a useful and legitimate role for interim housing and for various forms of recovery housing. In the US, we see a recent reframe of homelessness to a public health perspective. In the words of the new US Interagency Council on Homelessness (USICH) executive director, Jeffry Olivet, "the causes of homelessness are systemic, not individual." (PIElink [g] (n.d.).

In Canada, even some years earlier, we heard talk of "systemic HF," (Housing First) that is, to see permanent housing with voluntary support as the long-term aspiration for individuals, but with many other forms of constructive intervention possible, besides "pure" HF practice, on the road to get there from here (Nichols & Doberstein, 2016).

This shift means that these countries too are now looking for a broader framework of ideas and practice to bring a bigger vision to this work. A far broader account of the causes and solutions to homelessness needs a new language to get to the essence of the issues, and to the common ground of concern to do better, to work better together. It is too soon to say whether the PIE approach may be able to cross the Atlantic and play a useful part in this development. But it's a dialogue worth continuing to open.

Extending Beyond, to Other Fields of Complex Needs

These ideas, which were bubbling up and coming together at first in the new-found enthusiasm and sophistication of homelessness services, are now being found useful and being applied in a wider range of services for those with complex psychological and emotional needs.

Even in 2018, when it was being formulated, the revised PIEs framework, PIEs 2, saw this coming, and we took care to describe the essential concepts—the "Big Five" and the fifteen more specific practice elements—in a way that did not solely refer to homelessness. (PIElink [f], (n.d). Just as the precepts of pretreatment and trauma-informed care can be applied far more widely, the PIE approach is also potentially broad.

This means that other services facing other needs are free to explore what this spirit and this framework may have to offer them in addressing the complexity of needs in their own sphere. It is this breadth that then allows us to talk to each other, to develop the same awareness across platforms. This is necessary when our work requires us to find a shared vision of progress, one that bridges our areas of work, rather than the siloed thinking that has been part of the problem in the past.

Extending Upward to the Policy Makers

As our understanding of 'the environment' widens, we come to the idea that the systems we work within are themselves social constructions. In their own way, they are also "built environments," and they create the "social spaces" services must work within.

This last new direction for this dynamic new thinking may then prove to be more radical still. It is the need to communicate this enthusiasm and this commitment, and the lessons learned in services, up the chains of command, to policy makers and funders, even at national level.

Lately we have been hearing the claim that we do now know how to improve services, even within the severe resource constraints that we must live with. We have a growing sense of how to make these environments of all kinds more constructive. But now it seems to be the wider system in which all our work must operate that we must tackle.

This then brings with it a potential step change in thinking about what the full scope in the PIE approach might be. On the PIElink itself, there are pages asking whether, at some point, we might even want a new version of the PIE language, which takes these same ideas on what works, on what we are learning and what we now need, up another level. (PIElink[h], n.d).

This might mean another version of the PIEs framework that re-casts these ideas for a more extensive policy shift—in effect, a PIEs 3. Or it may be that the PIE approach and the PIE spirit that underlies it may need something else entirely, a still wider coalition of the positive voices and the messages we hear, when governments listen to service providers and service users.

Further Pathways

Both Pretreatment and PIEs, in their different spheres, have articulated the core issues and skills in engagement. Pretreatment looks mainly at the microsocial level of 1-1 interactions, and asks us to fully respect the subjective, experiential world of the individual, to engage first and foremost with "where they are at." The PIEs approach by comparison looks mainly at the meso-social level where organisations operate, and then asks us to consider every aspect of a service, to ask how far it helps us to deliver the engagements and the transitions we hope to see.

It might then seem that the PIEs approach is asking us to see the inner world of service users from the outside, but it is not. It is asking us to use our own natural capacity for empathy, to relate and connect, just as Pretreatment asks us to consider the ecology of issues for the individual, to respect their own investment in the environment of their lived experience—their "Umwelt." This is co-production on a 1-1 scale.

Nor does Pretreatment ignore the environment. A passage in *Cross-cultural Dialogues (Levy & Johnson, 2018, p. 228)* sums this up well:

"Similar to PIE, the term 'environment' is defined broadly and encompasses not only the physical environment, but also interpersonal aspects, exposure to ideas, values and rules that govern social structure, other participants, and even the different phases of a client-worker relationship."

At times of change, when we may be assisting someone in what we hope will be a successful transition and adaptation to new relationships, ideas, services, resources, treatment and housing, we must be most aware of what Jay calls "ecological considerations."

But what this alerts us to is that these considerations were in fact already there, for each individual, before we attempt to make contacts and offer new possibilities and opportunities. As Jay puts it in an earlier book: "*It is remarkable to think that my offer of help can easily be seen as disruptive or unsettling to their survival routines*." (p. 49, italics in the original, in *Pretreatment Guide to Homeless Outreach and Housing First*)

Pretreatment calls for a heightened sensitivity to the hidden costs for the individual of the changes we ask them to make. Simply ignoring these to focus solely on the outcomes the service is contracted to deliver may be the major reason for failure of a contact, a treatment programme, or a tenancy.

But now we need to explore how far we can go in using the PIEs approach and framework in looking upward at whole systems; and we look further still, at the macro-social world of policies and policy makers, politicians and opinion formers, influencers of all kinds in professional bodies, regulators and the information services.

There is also a still wider environment in which humanity struggles to find better ways to tackle the huge problems that are largely of our own making. Where and how we can ever hope to translate these values, insights and energies into a still more ambitious vision remains a moot point.

But we live in hope.

References

Boland, L (2018) *Transitioning from homelessness into a sustained tenancy: What enables successful tenancy sustainment?* (The Moving on Project) University of Plymouth Research Theses; http://hdl.handle.net/10026.1/11660

Cummings, F (n.d.) : Introduction to Umwelt theory and Biosemiotics, YouTube video: https://www.youtube.com/watch?v=G_0jJfliUvQ

Hattersley, C (2018) *Women At The Well*; presentation at Pathways national conference.

Johnson, R (2023a) *Psychologically Informed Environments from the ground up: service design for complex needs* : Fertile Imagination Press, Falmouth

Johnson, R (2023b) "The Window of Tolerance, the Drama Triangle and the Adjacent Possible" in : *Unfinished business : essays on the psychologically informed environment.* Fertile Imagination Press, Falmouth

Kull, K, (2001). Jakob von Uexküll: An introduction, in *Semiotica* 134 (1/4): 1-59

Levy, J. S. (2010). *Homeless narratives & pretreatment pathways: From words to housing*. Ann Arbor, MI: Loving Healing Press.

Levy, J. S. (2013). *Pretreatment guide for homeless outreach & Housing First: Helping couples, youth, and unaccompanied adults*. Ann Arbor, MI: Loving Healing Press.

Levy, J. S. & Johnson, R. (2018). *Cross-cultural dialogues on homelessness: From pretreatment strategies to psychologically informed environments*. Ann Arbor, MI: Loving Healing Press.

Levy, J. S. (2021). *Pretreatment in action: Interactive exploration of homelessness to housing stabilization*. Ann Arbor, MI: Loving Healing Press.

Nichols, N. & Doberstein, C. (2016) *Exploring effective systems responses to homelessness*. (ebook, via Homeless Hib, Canada: https://www.homelesshub.ca/SystemsResponses)

NPR – African Proverb Origins: https://www.npr.org/sections/goatsandsoda/2016/07/30/487925796/it-takes-a-village-to-determine-the-origins-of-an-african-proverb

PIElink [a] (n.d) : www.pielink.net

PIElink [b] (n.d) : https://pielink.net/the-umwelt

PIElink [c] (n.d) : https://pielink.net/proxemics/

PIElink [d] (n.d.) : https://pielink.net/unfinished-business/

PIElink [e] (n.d) : https://pielink.net/top-to-toe-pie-embedding/

PIElink [f] (n.d). https://pielink.net/pies-2-0-the-basics/

PIElink [g] (n.d.): https://pielink.net/questions/american-pie/

PIElink [h], (n.d). (The PIE languages of the future)

Yong, E (n.d.) : *The hidden world of animal senses* (Royal Institution lecture) YouTube video. https://www.youtube.com/watch?v=dVPN165wz1Y

6 Pretreatment in Mental Health Case Management: Learning to Care for Ourselves and Others

Kate Shapiro

> Develop enough courage so that you can stand up for yourself and then stand up for somebody else.
>
> Maya Angelou (2014)

I abhor the title "case manager" as I don't believe that people are cases to be managed. Nonetheless, that was my title at many different agencies throughout the years. I wish I had been introduced to the Pretreatment Model during my first embrace of this mislabeled title. I encountered Pretreatment a few years into my career and I can honestly state that it preserved my ability to remain in the field and enhanced the quality of my work exponentially.

"Case Management" in the mental health field is distinct from other types of case management such as nurse case management, in that there is no prerequisite training for most of these roles. There are some case management roles that require a master's degree in mental health or social work, but the majority of positions require a bachelor's degree as the highest required educational degree. I have a bachelor's degree in English Literature and a law degree, neither of which provided me training or transferable skills in the field of case management. More than the lack of prerequisite training, of the numerous case management positions I have held, none had a clear methodology, values or ethics in which to implement the primary goals of the role:

- Support individuals struggling with mental health challenges.
- Assess and refer to needed community resources and services.

- Identify and surmount barriers to recovery.
- Promote healthier living.

Initial Client Meetings: Intakes and Assessments

Despite the lack of uniformity in most case management, one similarity exists in all roles: the requirement to complete some form of premade assessment with a client within the first month of work with them. The information in these assessments form the basis of the service or treatment plan that contain goals on which case management work is based. As simple as this proposition appears on paper, asking someone you recently began working with intimate details about their physical and mental health history and a myriad of other personal questions is a profoundly challenging task. This is only made more challenging by the pressures to complete the process within a quick time frame. Adding to the challenge are the barriers that brought individuals to engage with case management to begin with. In addition to extensive trauma histories (often including trauma experienced in the mental health system), many of my clients struggled with an array of other barriers that interfered with traditional intake meeting models such as significant anxiety that limited our meetings to only a few minutes at a time. The difficulty in performing this challenging intake was exacerbated by the lack of training and standards for best practices for engaging clients in these profoundly personal and invasive assessments. In response, I eventually developed my own system for performing assessments, which embraced a Pretreatment approach.

After completing too many assessments that resulted in negative interactions between me and my new clients, I soon realized the need to approach the work differently. Instead of beginning our meeting with assessment-based questions, I took a step back to focus first on the Pretreatment principles of engagement and common language development. This was done to build trust and better connect with the client's world. Before we jumped into the assessment, I would help orient clients by stating that we will need to complete some paperwork. I then had a conversation with them about their experiences with past assessments and often share my own discomfort with performing assessments *on* them, thereby suggesting that this could be a co-production. We then developed a plan for completing the assessment together.

These plans sometimes included breaking up the assessment into shorter parts and completing it over a series of meetings. Other examples of client requests and agreed-upon approaches include us walking while doing the assessment and not disrupting our connection by actively writing down their answers or my interpretations. The most important element of any assessment plan was maintaining the engagement or our trusting relationship for doing effective work with the client. With this as the main goal, utilizing a jointly created strategy to complete the assessment became paramount. Utilization of the Pretreatment Model can provide guidance to all case managers through this difficult process of completing an initial assessment and setting goals, while enhancing the case managers' experience of their work, reducing frustration, and likely create better outcomes. In fact, thinking in terms of the stages of Engagement and Common Language Development (Levy, 2013) while completing the assessment was one of the main tools that helped me master this difficult task.

Supervision

Case management supervision is another area where the Pretreatment Model can be extremely beneficial. The lack of clear standards for case management execution leads to vast differences in case management supervision based on the supervisor's training, expertise, and values. I had one supervisor early in my career who held an MSW and believed very strongly in more traditional roles of case manager and client. Her beliefs around firm boundaries were so strong that she reprimanded me for purchasing coffee with my own money for a client as a tool for engagement, as she believed that constituted a boundary violation. In contrast, a later supervisor had such a different stance on boundaries that she permitted me to introduce my dog to a client. This lack of clearly defined roles, standards and strategies for case managers and case management supervisors leads to a tremendous amount of inefficiency, confusion, wasted resources, and for me till I found Pretreatment, burnout.

I was not familiar with the Pretreatment Model when I began my work as a case manager in 2007. I had just moved to Western

Massachusetts and though I had worked with youth throughout much of my life, case management was my first experience working with adults, as well as with the Massachusetts mental health system. The learning curve was steep. I had to learn the systems I was tasked to help individuals navigate, while also managing my own emotions around learning and failing, and my transference and counter-transference with clients. I found that many of the charged emotions and symptoms my clients were experiencing and at times expressing were the outcome of systematic failures such as poverty and lack of resources. No one seemed to speak of these structural issues and instead placed the onus on the individuals I was tasked with serving. I often received conflicting messages around the role of a case manager from my supervisor and other clinical professionals, which gave me great confusion and anxiety. I felt compressed and lonely, unable to find space in the system for my own values and belief in compassionate care. These experiences corresponded with the experiences of my clients in these systems and beyond.

I can't imagine how different things would have been had I had the language of Pretreatment prior to these experiences. Even better, what would the experience be for the entire agency and clients if everyone embraced the Pretreatment model, from case managers to supervisors to the executive director? I will never know exactly what that would look like. Despite numerous case management and case management supervisor roles since then, I have never worked for an agency that adopted the Pretreatment model or any clearly articulated model for case management. What kept me in the field of case management without the Pretreatment model despite the chaos was that I found colleagues and occasional supervisors who held Pretreatment values. Together we were able to support and learn from one another through reflective practice. In the book, *Pretreatment In Action* (Levy, 2021, p. 116-117), this type of joint exploration is referred to as co-vision.

I was the supervisor of one of my first Pretreatment mentors, Sandy (I know, that sounds backward!). Jay Levy had previously supervised her and I have always wondered if she introduced me to Pretreatment before it became fully known to me via the literature. Prior to meeting Sandy, I often felt alone in my passion for relationship formation. She quickly cured that feeling and introduced me to a whole new level of relationship formation. I was running a program that assisted individuals with disabilities who were in eviction proceedings to retain their housing by obtaining services to remedy their lease violations. In essence, clients needed to work with their case manager in order to stay housed. Given this context, I assumed relationship formation would be less important compared to my prior roles. How wrong I was!

Sandy modeled for me the value of Relationship Formation and Common Language Development in all case management contexts. Whereas, I had assumed the coercive nature of the relationship increased individuals' motivation to connect with their case manager, Sandy demonstrated for me that instead an authoritarian relationship increased participants' fears and anxieties, thereby requiring greater connection and safety between the case manager and the client. Instead of binary conversations around boundaries, she would ask the question, "who does the boundary serve and why do you need it?" This led to richer discussions about client needs as well as my own. Sandy pushed me from seeing myself as the helper, which was all about me, to seeing everyone as having something to contribute. Instead of staying in the role of expert and teacher, I began to be more curious and embrace my role as a learner and co-creator. Clients had so much to share with me, from their stories to their skills. With greater flexibility around teaching and helping roles, I was able to level some of the power imbalance. Our work truly became a co-production!

Sandy's role as my case management mentor, with me as her supervisor, reinforced the parallel process of supervision that is so key to Pretreatment. Similar to shifting the power imbalance with clients by having them teach me things, Sandy and I shifted our power imbalances through her mentorship of me. My early experiences with Pretreatment through Sandy made me a better supervisor, and case manager. More importantly, without Sandy, the relationship we formed and the common language we constructed, I would not have had the internal infrastructure to maintain myself in the field of case management for as long as I did.

Case Management: From Measuring Outcomes to Embracing the Journey

I was formally introduced to the Pretreatment model in my case management work at a large state agency where I managed a caseload of twenty to twenty-five individuals with mental health diagnoses that substantially affected their daily living. Similar to prior case management roles, there was no consistent value system or methodology to guide case management work, leaving the case management approach dependent on the individual case manager and case management supervisor. Though my supervisors did not embrace the Pretreatment Model, the formal model provided me a language in which I could create a small community of colleagues who shared similar values and ethics about case management work. This community and the meaning the Pretreatment model gave to my work, sustained me in this position for five years.

As a high-achieving woman raised in New York City, prior to a formal introduction to the Pretreatment model, I measured the success of my case management work on the outcomes of clients. This value system was reinforced in most case management roles I occupied where I was praised for positive client outcomes and often questioned and shamed for negative client outcomes. The Pretreatment model shifted this paradigm for me both professionally and personally. Instead of measuring outcomes, I began to emphasize and measure the quality of my interventions based on contextual relationship factors, such as the strength of my connection with clients, my authenticity, my transparency about power imbalances and my efforts to adjust them.

My use of the Pretreatment model likely altered many clients' outcomes as the focus became more on their journey and less about my need for predetermined outcomes. I was regularly gifted with comments like, "Thanks, no one has ever really cared so much about what I want." Most importantly, with outcomes relegated to the sidelines, I was able to more readily enter the client's world to see the context of their whole life history better than I had previously. This shift was entirely brought about by the Pretreatment Model and best described by Levy (2021, p. 39):

> The greater our understanding of people within the context of their narratives, the more we can work with, rather than inadvertently working against their values, aspirations, and sense of meaning. Our hope is to widen the field of view, before narrowing our focus to mutually defined goals.

My work supporting Jill[15] in achieving her goal of independent living helps illustrate this Pretreatment value. When I met Jill, she was a twenty-year-old, Caucasian woman who had been involved in state systems throughout most of her life: from the Department of Children and Families to Special Education[16] in the public schools to the Juvenile Justice System and now this large state agency. I struggled to develop a rapport with Jill for longer than it took me to develop trust with most clients. She was distrustful of public systems and often shared her dislike for case managers.

Jill's primary articulated goal was to find independent housing and discontinue mental health services. I was assigned to work with her for many reasons, one of which was my background in affordable housing and ability to support individuals in finding and maintaining affordable housing. I was thrilled when we were able to locate an appropriate apartment for her and pass the tenant screening process, a difficult feat given her criminal history. I hoped that supporting her in obtaining this apartment would increase her trust and comfort with me and I felt extremely proud of my role in supporting her in this process.

Once moved into the apartment, she returned to using substances and inviting houseless individuals into the apartment, who caused disruptions in violation of the lease. Instead of the increased connection I had hoped for, she slowly stopped returning my calls and missed several meetings. She left numerous angry voicemails in which she fired me and chastised me in other ways. She then had an incident while intoxicated involving a weapon and her landlord, which resulted in housing court action. My previous work in eviction prevention initially led to my preoccupation with maintaining her tenancy. Moreover, with my ego so connected to her obtaining this apartment, it was initially difficult for me to imagine any other option than supporting her in maintaining it.

---

[15] As in all of the chapters, client names and facts about their circumstances are changed to ensure anonymity. Similarly, though all circumstances and interactions occurred with clients I worked with, I have combined the facts and circumstances of a number of different clients into amalgamated clients to protect anonymity.

[16] See Chapter 4 where Virginia Bilz reviews the multiple challenges of Special Education and how Pretreatment provides a helpful guide for her work.

Co-visioning sessions (reflective practice) with my colleagues helped me identify that ecological barriers for her in this particular apartment were intense and that living alone presented many challenges for her. Levy (2021, p. 57) defines Ecological Considerations as examining how a person has attained equilibrium or is at disequilibrium within their given environmental context with a focus on the process of transition and adaptation to new people and their surroundings. For Jill, living in a small apartment in a high density building within close proximity to other mental health clients was reminiscent to her of past hospitalizations. What I had missed when she identified independent living as her primary goal was something unsaid: that independent living meant not being reminded of her mental health diagnosis or her connection to mental health services. Moreover, the apartment was located right beside a bike path where at any time of day one would find a number of homeless men hanging out. These men would often cat call, which was a profoundly triggering experience for Jill who had also a history of sexual trauma. These men often made her feel unsafe and she coped with that lack of safety by inviting others into her house to make her feel safer.

Co-visioning also reminded me that this housing experience was not a failure for her or me, but instead information for our next attempt to support her in achieving her housing goals. The backing I received from my colleagues was critical in identifying the boundaries and barriers I was unconsciously imposing on my work. Instead of a failure framework, I returned to the principles of relationship formation: connection, respect, curiosity, mutual learning, and consistency. Counterintuitive yet evident due to our co-vision sessions, the apartment was not vital to our maintained connection. My ability to be consistent and present in the face of the housing crisis was paramount to our relationship, more important than any singular apartment.

Jill was eventually hospitalized, during which time she detoxed from substances. Once she was more cogent and willing to speak to me, I took a very different approach than my natural inclination. Instead of me telling her how we could work to keep her apartment, I presented her with an array of options and we discussed what came up for her in each one of the possibilities. I gave her the power of information and choice and through that interaction, our relationship remained intact. She ended up choosing to leave the apartment in order to avoid eviction.

I believe the way that she and I framed the decision to relinquish the apartment as a choice and not as a failure empowered her to take greater ownership and responsibility for future housing decisions. My commitment to work with her despite her behavior toward me while living there was the foundation for a more trusting, richer relationship between us. Jill and I worked together for many years after that first apartment. She experienced another similarly tumultuous apartment placement, but remained engaged with case management services and ultimately found an apartment that had the ecological factors that better fit her needs. Upon my departure from this position, Jill remained in that apartment with needed support and renewed hope for a better future.

During our final meeting, Jill thanked me for teaching her how she deserved to be treated. She indicated that no one in her life had ever been as kind, respectful and consistent and that she would use our relationship as a basis to measure acceptable behavior toward her in the future. I cried that day and cry as I recount the story. It is an incredible gift and honor to be able to positively affect someone's life in that way, and even more rare to have them acknowledge your impact. I will always be grateful to Jill for allowing me to love and care for her for so many years. I'm thankful to Sandy and Pretreatment for helping me find that gift in Jill and myself.

Anna: Hearing Her Voice

Pretreatment's focus on relationships, common language and the Stages of Change (Prochaska & DiClemente, 1982) also helped me manage my own anxiety and distress when placed in situations where I had minimal power. My work with a young woman named Anna illustrates this benefit of Pretreatment. One of my first visits with Anna took place at a long-term inpatient hospital she had resided in for over two years. She was a Hispanic woman originally from South America who was a devout Catholic, a very different background from my own. During our initial visit, she spent the entire meeting listing out to me in an elevated voice many problems with the hospital and the poor treatment she'd received.

This interaction initially elicited extreme emotions in me. First, having spent a significant amount of time with other clients at that hospital, I agreed with many of her complaints, but did not have the power to change anything at the hospital; I felt obligated to help solve these barriers but knew I did not have the agency to do so. Additionally, I initially experienced her loud voice volume as screaming at me, which was based on my own trauma. Luckily for me, the co-visioning work I had done with colleagues provided me the space to understand her communication differently and provided me with a framework to calm myself down. Instead of my habit of trying to fix the problems at the hospital for her, I listened with a closer ear to what she was saying and why she was speaking so loudly. After a while, I asked her if she had spoken to anyone else about her complaints. She indicated that she had, but that no one listened to what she was saying and instead she was labeled as being "escalated" and often redirected to quiet down. I replied to her "so you just want someone to hear you?" to which she concurred loudly and emphatically with her whole body.

I assumed she not only wanted someone to hear her, but someone in power. Despite my experience of powerlessness, as a Case Manager of a large state agency, I represented power for her. We had reached a common language, at least for that day. Freed from my own need to fix everything, I was able to sit with her for a full hour and just listen to her and try to understand where she was coming from. The success was making a connection and listening close enough to hear what she was trying to communicate. At the end of the meeting, we discussed potential action steps to remediate the problems, but she declined to consider them. She wasn't ready to begin discussing improving her hospital experience or more importantly what she needed to do to exit the hospital.

The stages of change model helped shape that insight. Anna was contemplative of her presenting problems, though not yet ready to pursue change. So instead of an action step, Anna and I worked on getting to know each other better. We developed a greater sense of trust and improved communication. Upon her request, I was able to get her a pass to leave the hospital and we went on an outing where I discovered her love of pop music. She and I connected around this joint passion, and I began bringing music with me when visiting her. Despite being offered a spot at a group living environment upon discharge from the hospital, Anna chose to return to her family's house with significant support services. This arrangement did not last long and unfortunately

Anna was re-hospitalized and ultimately returned to long term hospitalization. Nevertheless, the critical connection Anna and I made during her first hospitalization laid the groundwork for our continued work. After that initial meeting, we worked together for many years. A journey at her pace of experiencing, seeing and learning that eventually led to addressing many of her stated concerns, rather than being focused on my preconceived agenda.

Conclusion

The work mental health case managers perform, supporting individuals who are struggling and in crisis, is profoundly challenging regardless of the framework used to guide the work. The Pretreatment Model supported me in aligning this work with my personal values, but it did not make the work easier. It remains profoundly challenging for me to abandon my sense of control and self-generated ideas of purpose, and adopt a model of exploration of relationship and shared power as is required for Pretreatment work. This discomfort was exacerbated by the frequent challenges I received to my Pretreatment-oriented work from colleagues and leaders who adhered to more traditional clinical roles and the data systems that were blind to my good work.

Why would I continue to utilize a framework that challenged me in an already difficult role? I use Pretreatment because it is the best modality I have come across for performing the difficult work of mental health case management. I believe in Pretreatment because it led me through the process of my work with Jill, Anna and many others, while experiencing all the beauty of those relationships. Jill never had to thank me for finding her housing or supporting her through a number of other crises. She did not need to. Those accomplishments were not the most important part of our work together. At the end of our lives, neither she nor I will remember the specific goals we accomplished. We will remember the care we felt towards each other. That was our most profound achievement.

> This chapter is dedicated to Sandy Haigh, my mentor and friend. May you rest easier knowing that your mentorship saved the world from another Muffy.

References

Angelou, M. (2014) rainbow in the cloud: the wisdom and spirit of maya angelou. New York: Random House.

Levy, J. S. (2013). *Pretreatment guide for homeless outreach & housing first: Helping couples, youth, and unaccompanied adults*. Ann Arbor, MI: Loving Healing Press.

Levy, J. S. (2021). *Pretreatment in action: Interactive exploration of homelessness to housing stabilization*. Ann Arbor, MI: Loving Healing Press.

Prochaska, J.O. & DiClemente, C.C. (1982). Trans theoretical therapy: Toward a more integrative model of change. *Psychotherapy: Theory, Research, and Practice*. 19, 276-288.

7 High Windows and Lost Souls: Trauma and Homelessness in Hull

Chris Brown and Dan Southall

They fuck you up, your Mum and Dad.
They don't mean to, but they do
They fill you with all the faults they had,
And add some extra just for you.

But they were fucked up in their turn
By fools in old style hats and coats,
Who half the time were soppy-stern
And half at one another's throats.

Man hands on misery to man.
It deepens like a coastal shelf.
Get out as early as you can,
And don't have any kids yourself.

Philip Larkin, 1971

PART ONE: Setting The Scene

Introduction

Philip Larkin wrote his poem during his tenure as librarian at the University of Hull—the role he held for most of his career until his death in 1985. Whilst many might see Larkin's poem as a parable of misery and hopelessness, we see it more as it was intended—a statement of acceptance that, as humans, we can cause immeasurable suffering to each other, but that suffering is not inflicted intentionally and is purely the unfortunate consequence of being part of a family.

We also think of Larkin's poem as an insight into what it is like to be a resident of Hull, at least for some. A once successful and thriving city, it has been scarred by industrial decline and economic austerity. Families here are proud, but are often struggling with the effects of poverty, adversity, and neglect. Many of the people we support are the product of families that have fallen on hard times, feel unsupported by society, and have suffered the terrible consequences of interfamilial abuse and developmental trauma. It seems that, at the time that our team began working with them, nobody had made the connection between the environment they had grown up in and the fact that they were homeless.

We provide here a frank, open and honest account of our journey and the development of our team—a narrative of its inception, with the gaps in our knowledge around the impact of psychological trauma, and the mistakes we made. We hope it conveys the difficult learning moments that helped us develop our understanding of the path we were to follow, how we learned to understand psychological trauma and our efforts to integrate Pre-treatment therapy with other clinically relevant psychological approaches.

Life in Hull[17]

Hull is a city with much to be proud of. A thriving centre of industry and tourism in the north of England, Hull is a gateway to Europe, with a busy port, several multinational healthcare companies, the home of two professional rugby league teams (the only city in the northern hemisphere to claim this title!), and a former world-leader in the fishing industry. Many parts of the city, including the Old Town, Humber Street, and the Pearson Park district, contribute to Hull being one of the best locations for a night out in the UK. The University of Hull is a highly ranked centre for higher education and boasts exceptional student experience ratings. The beautiful Yorkshire Wolds are merely a stone's throw away, and award-winning seaside resorts including Bridlington, Hornsea, and Filey are only a short drive up the coast.

Many aspects of the city's identity have been lost now, following the decline of the fishing industry and the closure of many of the docks, leading to the end of much of its long maritime history. This loss of

[17] See links to **Life in Hull Corresponding Data Sources* in Reference section.

identity has contributed to some of the city's social difficulties. Sadly, the city struggles against its reputation as one of the most dangerous places to live in the UK.[18] The crime rate in Hull has increased steadily over the last decade, with violent incidents increasing by 62%.[19] Although there have been some improvements recently with an increase in policing,[20] Hull still ranks as the most dangerous place to live in the East Riding (East Yorkshire), with violent and sexual offences being the most common crimes.[21] Often thought of as a bit of a lost cause,[22] Hull was ranked fourth on a national metric of UK cities with the highest number of deprived neighbourhoods.[23]

Deprivation and lack of hope can make it difficult for the population of a city to care for itself, and Hull suffers from poor health outcomes relative to the rest of the country. Hull has some of the highest rates of mental health difficulties in England, with low rates of life satisfaction. About 10% of adults have accessed services for support with depression and anxiety, while admission to hospital and risk of early death due to drug and alcohol use are higher than the rest of the country.[24] Problematic drug and alcohol use is rife; Hull has some of the highest numbers of opiate users in the United Kingdom.[25]

Poverty, mental health, and substance misuse are just some of the issues contributing to homelessness in Hull, which has also increased in the city, with the number of rough sleepers now between sixty and seventy, the highest numbers since the onset of Covid-19 in early 2020. Between eighty and 100 people return to sleep rough on a frequent basis (Dowson, 2022). There are often around 350 individuals housed in the city's homelessness hostels and in short-term accommodation, although

---

[18] https://www.hulldailymail.co.uk/news/uk-world-news/crime-map-ranks-most-dangerous-8191037

[19] https://www.varbes.com/crime/kingston-upon-hull-city-of-crime

[20] https://www.hulldailymail.co.uk/news/hull-east-yorkshire-news/crime-rising-humber-police-well-8967668

[21] https://crimerate.co.uk/east-riding-of-yorkshire/kingston-upon-hull

[22] https://www.theguardian.com/uk-news/the-northerner/2013/jul/19/top-10-myths-about-hull

[23] https://data.hull.gov.uk/wp-content/uploads/Briefing-Report-Hull-English-Indices-of-Deprivation-2019.pdf

[24] https://commonslibrary.parliament.uk/research-briefings/sn06988/

[25] https://www.hulljsna.com/adults/lifestyle-factors-adults/drugs-adults.

this has reduced since 2023 following the unfortunate closure of one of the city's (and England's) largest hostels, William Booth House.

The Emergence of Hull's Homeless Mental Health Team

The Humber Homeless Mental Health Team was commissioned as part of a city-wide initiative to work in partnership with other local organisations to provide mental health support for homeless people in the city.

The publication of the Homeless Reduction Act in 2017 significantly changed the way that local authorities, health services and third-sector providers think about and work with homelessness in their towns and cities. The act called upon all local authorities in England to take more responsibility for preventing and relieving homelessness, in part by addressing the factors that lead to homelessness and housing issues. As homelessness increased in Hull, a partnership between local NHS (National Health Service) organisations and council bodies came together to look for solutions for the increasing problems.

The Humber Homeless Mental Health Team emerged in Winter 2019, a few months prior to the start of the Covid-19 pandemic and the subsequent national lockdown. Prompted by the publication of the Homeless Reduction Act, the service was a joint venture co-financed by NHS England, Hull City Council, and the local NHS mental health trust.

The aims of the service were simple: provide mental health assessment and treatment to individuals who were sleeping rough, accommodated in one of the city's homeless hostels, or were precariously housed. Referrals were welcomed from a range of local partners including Hull City Council, the police, mental health crisis team, and directly from the hostels. We were instructed to remove inclusion and exclusion criteria and make the service as accessible as we could. People could self-refer for input simply by approaching us, and they would not be refused if they attended under the influence of drugs or alcohol.

The mental health trust we worked for had never seen a team or a service like ours. Most other adult mental health services were nurse-led and overseen by a consultant psychiatrist making most of the clinical decisions. We were a team led mainly by social workers and a psychologist, working together. People were sceptical about how successful we were likely to be, and we subsequently learned that people we worked with were saying that we would probably fail within the first year.

First Steps

Our first meetings with homeless people were a huge wake-up call. Although we had all worked in secondary care mental health services with people with severe and enduring mental health difficulties for many years prior to joining the team, we were completely unprepared for the level of distress and sense of social marginalisation we encountered. We had done some prior research, and were aware of the high levels of depression, anxiety, and experiences of childhood neglect and abuse in the homeless population (Rees, 2009), and as we dug further into the literature, we learned of the high prevalence of "personality disorder" diagnoses in homeless people (Keats, Maguire, Johnson, & Cockerell, 2012).

Many of us had little or no previous experience of working with homeless communities, so our first forays into working with our client base provided us with many opportunities to learn about their traumatic experiences and how they can affect people. Although we knew we would be working with people with histories of trauma, we were certainly unprepared for the range of psychological, emotional, and social difficulties people presented with.

The level of anger we faced when we met people was overwhelming. Looking back now, we were very naïve about the huge variety of ways that trauma symptoms can present in homeless people, and still had a long way to go before we could be able to carefully and skilfully assess how a person's lived and living experiences impacted on them. A constant sense of threat and chaotic lifestyles seemed to go hand in hand, as people seemed constantly anxious and paranoid about other people in their lives. They talked at length about how they felt persecuted by people in positions of power such as hostel managers, doctors, probation workers, and housing organisations. There appeared to be a constant state of "fight or flight" for many people, and attempting to manage this using alcohol, illicit drugs, prescription medication, or all three led to difficulties maintaining housing or stable accommodation. People seemed to feel dismissed by healthcare professionals and criticised for struggling to stop using substances or not taking care of themselves, which exacerbated their other existing health conditions.

We heard about people's considerable difficulties maintaining relationships with their families, and often their homelessness was a result of turmoil in the family, rejection, domestic violence, and/or relationships that could not withstand the lifestyles they seemed to choose. Many were parents who had lost contact with their children or were prevented doing so by court orders. They were seldom in employment and could not maintain health treatment of any kind.

Early Learning from our First Year

We drew on all forms of guidance, support, and mentoring offered to us. We emailed, video called, and spoke to anyone with expertise in working psychologically with homelessness. Robin Johnson told us that we would "bumble around for the first two years before you understand what the task is." Another learned colleague later pointed out that typical psychological approaches such as cognitive-behavioural therapy and acceptance and commitment therapy were often either simply unhelpful or at worst damaging for the homeless population.

Standard mental health approaches for engaging people and supporting them were fruitless with this population. We received referrals for people struggling with their mental health, arranged to meet with them for assessment and didn't see them again for months. We would begin our standard mental health assessment and attempt to explore the main problems, the circumstances in which the current problem had developed and background issues that might underpin their difficulties. They often seemed fine talking to us initially, but unbeknownst to us at the time, found the process very distressing (see Matt Bennett's discussion of intake in chapter 2). We soon realised that we were subjecting people to the assessment process that they had been exposed to in other settings, which often retraumatised or rejected them.

With some of the people we worked with in the early days, we often developed very good therapeutic relationships and began to think about how things could be different for them. We tried lots of different psychosocial interventions such as anxiety management and emotion regulation skills to negligible effect. Unbeknownst to us at the time, numerous challenges and obstacles caused stress and upheaval for the people we worked with and made any meaningful progress slow. They were dealing with regular conflict with well-meaning hostel staff, rejection and disappointment in existing relationships, and contact with the criminal justice system and other services. We learned that these approaches were not helping people solve day-to-day problems or manage their relationships.

Other mental health services such as hospital-based liaison teams, inpatient psychiatric wards, and community mental health teams often found homeless people too chaotic to care for and discharged them very quickly; their distress during reassessment was perceived as unwillingness to engage with staff. This led to frustration on the part of healthcare professionals but, most importantly, hopelessness and a sense of mistrust on the part of service users. People admitted to wards gave extensive histories of stressful, abusive, and neglectful childhoods that were often not even considered in treatment plans. They found standard psychiatric care dismissive and retraumatising and were often discharged from wards or left of their own volition without appropriate or realistic ongoing care options. Homeless people often had highly negative experiences of healthcare services and psychiatry in particular; they received diagnoses (mental and behavioural disorder secondary to substance misuse was a common one) that did not reflect the debilitating and deleterious environments they had grown up in or were embedded in now. This left them feeling labelled, dismissed, understandably angry, and had ongoing mistrust of services.

Our mentors were correct. We learned many practical lessons in the first two years simply by trying to encourage homeless people to talk to us. We didn't know anything about trauma-informed practice, and we knew nothing about Pre-treatment therapy at this point. These first two years in operation highlighted some of the gaps in our knowledge. We realised that we needed an original approach to allow us to engage Hull's homeless community and develop a good understanding of people's difficulties without alienating them. We also felt that we needed to combine a simple approach to engagement with existing theories of motivation, change, and therapeutic approaches to working with traumatised people.

Reflections: Drop-ins

Adapting drop-ins at hostels was a major issue when I started working with the team approximately two years ago. No doubt coming from a good place, staff would often "drag in" people who didn't want to speak or insist that I go up to their room and knock at the door. I remember very early on, Dan (psychologist) explaining that if a person knew there was an informal drop-in on, and chose not to come, then they were "voting with their feet" and that I should be respectful of that—and I've carried this with me ever since.

I continually look to adapt the drop-in itself, based on the hostel environment, residents, and staff. For example, at another hostel in the city where space is tight, I tend to have a brief, private chat with residents in a quiet corner only when we know each other, or they've told staff they'd like to, before arranging to chat elsewhere (usually the pavement for a walk around the block/to the shops) within the next few minutes, or another time more convenient to them.

Forming the relationship is done by looking to reduce power, flattening the hierarchy, and, often, by not talking about "mental health" at all, but by genuinely engaging with them as people and their experiences. A sound reputation goes a long way, and people have approached me and said that they had heard I was "alright" from one of their peers who I may be, or had been, working with. No doubt, people talk about the support they receive and whether it is valuable to them or not.

Always, it is about people's right to confidentiality, anonymity, and respect, without compromise.

Chris, Social Worker

Reflections: Traditions

I am mindful of the conventional settings at play. Yes, I go to the person where they want to meet and in their timeframe, but an awareness of the impact of cultural and ecological considerations is also important. Space and timing are paramount, so I need to be flexible about time and location. I may walk around or sit somewhere, speaking with people generally. This encourages them to speak to me, then, if we can find a safe space to meet, or later on for however long they'd like. While this approach is obviously far from perfect, it is an improvement from sitting in a room, waiting for a knock at the door, and for a person and/or staff member to enter as if it's a GP appointment or worse.

Chris, Social Worker

PART TWO: Putting It All Together

Understanding Complex Trauma

Our first major challenge was to really develop an understanding of the difficulties homeless people were struggling with. They had received various diagnoses including mental and behavioural disorder, emotionally unstable personality disorder, paranoid schizophrenia, attention deficit hyperactivity disorder, and a range of others. Homeless people often have trouble in receiving the correct mental health diagnosis (Hertzberg & Boobis, 2022). An overwhelming majority of homeless people—somewhere in the region of 65 to 80%—have faced frightening and neglectful childhoods and adult lives filled with rejection, marginalisation, and maltreatment (Maguire, 2012; Irving & Harding, 2022). This is why many people presented with highly complex mental health difficulties and why we considered these difficulties to fit what we currently call *complex trauma* or *complex post-traumatic stress disorder*.

Individuals with post-traumatic stress disorder often experience a range of symptoms including reexperiencing the traumatic event in the form of flashbacks or dreams, avoidance of both the memory itself and triggers associated with reminders of the trauma, and difficulties with mood such as detachment, irritability, or absence of positive emotion (Bryant, 2019). Survivors of developmental trauma, child abuse, incest, neglect, and other distressing interpersonal experiences often experience these symptoms as well as a significant number of other problem areas (Courtois, 2008). These additional symptoms include disturbances in sense of self, difficulties in emotional regulation, and difficulties in sustaining relationships (Courtois & Ford, 2012). We reduced the concept to an easily assessed set of three core problems: Cognitive and Emotional Difficulties, Relationship or Interpersonal Difficulties, and Difficulties with Identity and Self (see Table 7-1, p. 119). Our colleague and mentor, John Conolly, refers to this in the homeless community as "traumatised personality."

With more of an understanding of their needs, we began to take a slower approach to assessment to develop an ongoing story of that person's difficulties and understanding of what has happened to them. We continued to note that people found it difficult to engage in structured assessments and preferred to work with us over the course of several drop-in sessions that we could offer in a more informal manner. It still took us some time, though, to realise that we needed to reassess our intervention work, and develop a simple framework for engaging traumatised, disconnected people—indeed, not rushing in and "doing" is still an ongoing professional dilemma.

Table 7-1. Simplified Conceptualisation of C-PTSD.

Type of difficulty	Description of difficulty
Emotion regulation and consciousness	A constant feeling of dread that something bad might happen. Explosive or overly inhibited anger. Dissociation—depersonalisation, derealisation, disconnection. Reliving, flashbacks, nightmares, rumination. Constant threat—"fight or flight." Brief psychotic episodes and distressing voices. Concentration and cognitive difficulties.
Interpersonal difficulties	Fear of relationships. A need to be rescued. Splitting—others seen as either good (rescuers) or bad (perpetrators). Difficulty trusting people in positions of power and authority.
Problems with sense of identity and self	Ego shifts—rapid fluctuation between adult, child, or parent position. Feelings of difference from others, detachedness, aloneness. Sense of hopelessness and despair. Pervasive shame, guilt, and self-blame. A sense of everything being your fault.

Expanding Pretreatment

We were guided toward the Pretreatment Model (Levy, 2000; 2021) in our interactions with colleagues from around the country, and we immediately saw the possibilities that this approach opened to us. Pretreatment could be introduced as a simple, stepwise framework that could be employed by qualified and unqualified members of our team and workers in the field from other agencies. It provides guidance for becoming person-centred in our work by following five universal principles of care (See Jay Levy's description in chapters 1 and 3):

- Relationship Formation via the stages of pre-engagement, engagement, and contracting.
- Common Language Construction to develop improved communication by connecting to people's words, ideas, and values.
- Ecological Considerations that focus on the process of transition and adaptation to new (or changes with) people, relationships, ideas, and environments.

- Promoting Safety through Crisis Intervention and Harm Reduction strategies.
- Facilitating Change via the Stages of Change and Motivational Interviewing techniques.

Because the team was largely guided by psychological formulation, we needed to marry Pretreatment with an existing psychological evidence-based therapeutic model. We also included theories of trauma and motivation to guide our work. Three additional theories informed our adaptation of Pre-treatment therapy. We had very clear ideas of the steps of the approach when working with our model, but held in mind these ideas when engaging with, formulating and care planning for people. See Fig. 7-2 for a simplified depiction of our combined model.

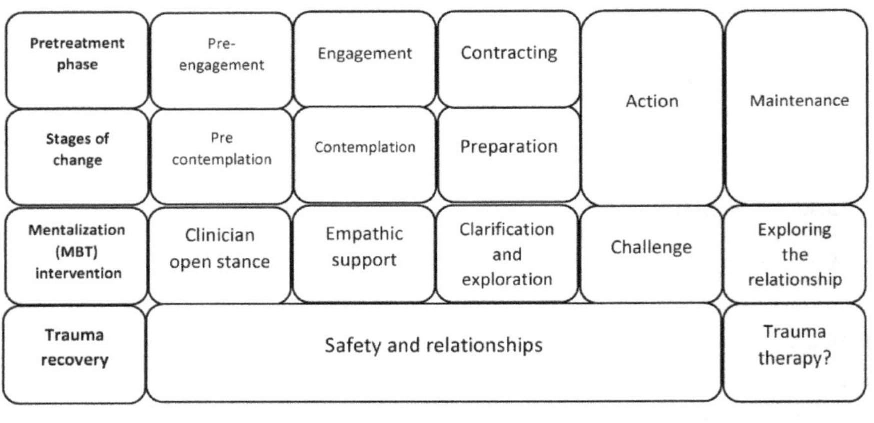

Fig. 7-2. Simplified phased approach to engagement and intervention, combining Pretreatment with other therapeutic approaches.

Transtheoretical Model of Behaviour Change

We worked hard to ensure that we tailored our interventions to meet people's needs. Changing an unhelpful coping strategy is undeniably difficult, especially when you seldom feel safe in your own body, let alone in your living environment. Many of those we supported were often guided by overwhelming emotions, and they often had very little consistent support to make changes. Therefore, we recognised that it was us that needed to be mindful of the challenges, be united and equal with people in helping them set achievable goals and be present to support them through the failures.

For this reason, we incorporated the Transtheoretical Model of Behaviour Change (Prochaska & DiClemente, 1983), often referred to as "stages of change." According to the model, behaviour change is thought to involve a series of stages (Norcross, Krebs, & Prochaska, 2011):

- **Precontemplation**—Individuals are not ready to take action and may be unaware that their behaviour causes them issues. People around the individual are often well aware of the behaviour and its consequences.
- **Contemplation**—Individuals are beginning to recognize that their behaviour causes issues and are getting ready to think about how to change it.
- **Preparation**—Individuals are ready to take action and may start taking small steps toward change.
- **Action**—Individuals have made efforts to modify the problem behaviour in spite of barriers over a period between a day and six months.
- **Maintenance**—In this stage, individuals have maintained new behaviours for a period of six months or more and are working to prevent relapse into old behaviours.

Consideration of the Transtheoretical Model and careful assessment in session of the person's current position enabled us to carefully adjust the focus of the conversation and avoid mistakes in session, for example ensuring that we did not move to consider what behaviour needed to change or how it could change too quickly, and instead supporting them to think about the problem in depth before moving on.

Herman's Stages of Recovery from Trauma

We drew upon Judith Herman's three-stage model of recovery from psychological trauma she developed in her work with people with complex trauma reactions (Herman, 1992; 1998). Again, the addition of this theory enabled us to be clear in the direction of our work, carefully selecting interventions and focusing on the development of safe and trusting relationships. Herman argued that recovery from trauma occurred in three stages.

The first stage focuses on creating safety. This involves an initial focus on physical safety—a secure living environment, safety planning, financial security, and such—before moving on to emotional, psychological, and relational safety. Only after the tasks of creating safety have been completed can the worker and service user consider moving on to stage two—processing—which involves psychological therapy to address traumatic memories and emotions. Once the person has been supported to tell their story and come to terms with their memories, they move on to stage three, the focus of which is meaning and reconnection, helping them to develop stronger and more supportive relationships and considering what might come next in their lives.

Many of our colleagues around the city believed that our aim was to provide psychological therapy, but we considered our role as largely focusing only on the first stage of recovery. We often talked in meetings and discussions about the work of understanding the interaction between safety and threat for each individual and working only on the tasks of being empathic, creating and planning safety for them. We seldom provided trauma therapy, and only did so when individuals had moved to established housing, had developed some skills for managing distress and had discussed more intensive therapy with their worker.

Mentalization-Based Treatment

The innovation that we are most proud of in our adaptation of Pre-treatment therapy is the addition of mentalization-based treatment (MBT) to the process. Augmenting our work with MBT allowed us to develop collaborative psychological formulations based on an evidence-based therapeutic approach specifically aimed at people with relational difficulties and complex emotional needs. It also helped us to add some straightforward therapeutic interventions that enabled us to manage moments of high distress and focus on developing the therapeutic relationship.

Mentalization-based treatment (MBT) is a form of psychological therapy specifically for people with diagnoses or difficulties associated with borderline personality disorder (Bateman & Fonagy, 2010). Mentalization itself is the ability to understand the thoughts, feelings and motivations of ourselves and others. It is a crucial process for the successful functioning of social relationships. High (or good) mentalizing allows us to reflect on what motivates others, and an ability, to some degree, to understand what emotional and cognitive processes might have influenced their behaviour. Poor mentalizing means that we make mistakes in these inferences, which leads to high levels of interpersonal difficulty and emotional distress (Bateman & Fonagy 2016).

Mentalization is a developmental process that develops and is nurtured through attachment relationships. It depends upon the presence of a safe and caring adult who can appropriately recognise and understand emotional states and reflects this back to the child through a mirroring process and modelling an appropriate emotional response (Bateman & Fonagy, 2019). Of course, the absence of these safe and nurturing relationships is catastrophic for mentalizing, and when this is the case, it is more likely that the mind is closed to receiving new knowledge from others in the context of relationships, a process known as "epistemic mistrust." Mentalizing difficulties and epistemic mistrust are known to be caused by trauma, abuse, and neglect (Bateman et al., 2023).

Standard treatment involves psychoeducational groups followed by both individual and group treatment. The person receives a formulation collaboratively developed between themselves and the clinician, an alliance which enables them to understand when non-mentalizing processes are occurring and to think about specific goals for therapy (Bateman & Fonagy, 2016). We were of course not able to offer this type of treatment, but we were able to tailor our work with people relative to the course of interventions suggested in MBT treatment. We always begin by being both "boundaried" and available, making no specific promises but providing high levels of empathy and validation, and being supportive.

The aim of mentalization-based treatment is always to regain mentalizing when it is reduced or has been lost. In the context of homelessness, the triggers to loss of mentalizing are everywhere—conflict, attachment distress, physical attack, exclusion, rejection, loss of accommodation—the list is endless. The clinician's stance is crucial to the process of mentalizing; the individual is the expert in understanding their own mind, not the clinician, and we explore their experience from a position of "not-knowing." We make no attempt to determine or insert the correct sequences of events, we are only interested in the course of events and how they made sense of them.

One reason that mentalization was a complimentary approach to Pretreatment is that the process follows a trajectory of treatment: we do not tend to move on to a higher-level intervention until a lower-level intervention has been attempted, as the higher-level intervention is likely to fail.

As we allow the course of events to unfold, we ensure that we listen with empathy and validation for their experience. This does not mean that we agree with their position or any unhelpful coping behaviour. Rather, we see things from the individual's perspective and provide compassion and care for the way they have made sense of a situation. Mentalizing cannot be regained if the clinician is not mentalizing, and is judging or invalidating. As we move on, openly building the experience of the clinician as a compassionate "other mind" that is interested in their experience of a difficult situation, we begin to explore and "unpack" in more detail. We are keen to identify the point where mentalizing was lost and how the individual has made sense of the event.

For example, our colleagues elsewhere might be quick to try and correct behaviour amidst conflict and high distress; this is where we would acknowledge the distress and figuratively sit alongside them, reassuring and trying to understand the situation from their perspective. As distress reduces, we move to trying to understand the situation as it unfolded, working back over the incident, allowing the person to process their feelings, and understanding at what point they became overwhelmed and mentalizing was lost. Only when people feel safe with us and become more able to manage their distressing feelings do we begin to ask or perhaps gently challenge them to consider alternative perspectives. Only later, when some ability to mentalize has been established, does the clinician explore processes in the relationship itself, and to some degree, seeing if the individual can think about the clinician's mind and how each is making sense of the other.

PART THREE: In Practice

In this section, we introduce our approach to Pre-treatment Therapy using examples in practice. We begin by describing each step of Pretreatment in detail, and then some case examples.

Stage 1—Pre-engagement

The result of homelessness, trauma, and attachment difficulties is that our clients struggled to trust us and would respond to attempts to build relationships with threat emotions such as fear and anger (Theodorou, Johnsen, Watts, & Burley, 2021). The focus here is to begin to gently approach people, reduce sense of threat and gradually build up engagement.

We worked with countless individuals in Hull who, on first presentation, were mistrusting, hostile, and sometimes aggressive. On occasion people were dismissing and felt they did not need help. Our focus here was to build up engagement slowly, since many people could only tolerate thirty seconds of contact with professionals. Our role was to build that engagement up in this initial stage, from thirty seconds to a minute, to five minutes, to an hour.

Many homeless people we encountered were very reluctant to engage with us (as previously mentioned) due to previous experiences of services as judging or rejecting. People felt criticized or dismissed by mainstream services and this had caused intolerable, overwhelming feelings of shame, anger, and mistrust (Courtois, 2008; Fonagy, Luyten, Allison, & Campbell, 2017). It was fundamental to our early engagement to ensure that we did not repeat these kinds of experiences and we respected the diverse lived and living experiences people had/have.

Therefore, a strong emphasis is placed on good beginnings and the significance of early interactions. Underpinning our practice is an acknowledgement of the importance of the very first contact and interaction (be it a thirty second phone call or other) to make a positive contribution to begin to establish some rapport. We recommended slowly approaching the individual, often asking for consent—"is it OK if I come and talk to you?" or "have you got a minute to chat with me?" We felt it crucially important to be mindful of their personal space and that encroaching on that might increase mistrust and hostility. In hostels, people often found themselves being constantly reprimanded or addressed in condescending tones of voice, so it was crucial that we approach with a non-threatening tone of voice that did not create a position of power.

We found it crucially important to help people begin to solve practical problems here and meet their basic human needs. Access to dentist appointments, support to collect medication, charging mobile phones, connecting them with the benefits adviser—not only did this help people feel more settled but also increased a sense of trust in us that we were not going to dismiss, reject or cause harm and we were interested in them. "This person is safe, they will help me meet my needs and they will not harm me."

Because we were not formally providing mental health assessment in the early stages of our relationships, we focused instead on developing a thorough understanding of the individual's language style. Although people generally had their own idiosyncratic lexicon that we listened out for and noted, we were keen to understand the language through behaviour. What did it mean when someone did not remain in a room they had been offered? Why did they become so angry with certain council workers? Often this type of behaviour gave us very important clues to past experiences of exclusion, abandonment and mistreatment, and gave us key areas for intervention.

From here, we began to develop a script, understanding and mapping their experiences of other services—eviction from a hostel, being shamed in a meeting within an inpatient ward, experiences of power with substance misuse providers—so that we could ensure that we did not repeat previous relationships and could begin to rescript their experience of professionals.

Stage 2—Engagement

Considering safety continues to be paramount as engagement grows, particularly in terms of relational safety. We recognised the importance of relational safety as being the key factor in opening the doors to the prospect of change (Herman, 1992). We also understood that change is impossible when individuals continue to feel at risk of harm (Fonagy & Allison, 2014). In the engagement stage, with a trusting and therapeutic relationship developing, the goal is to continue to provide a safe space for someone who may be open to having a different kind of relationship but is not ready to make more significant changes.

The key in this stage is listening and validating. It does not require advanced therapeutic skills or specialist training. The focus should be on empathically and patiently giving space to hear the narrative of the person's life in the manner that they wish to express it, and bearing witness to it. We will occasionally say the wrong thing, unwittingly cause offence or distress, and have to support the individual through a personal crisis. The crucial point is that we make space for ruptures, apologise when we have made a mistake and show commitment to restoring and continuing with the relationship. We found that empathising, normalising, and validating were often alien experiences for people and allowed them to express distress in a safe environment.

As we move through this stage, and face all the instances of breakdowns, rejections, and resolution, we begin to support the individual to understand shameful behaviours as responses to trauma and contextualise interactions of conflict with others in a similar manner. For example, we reassure people not to feel compelled to detail their awful childhood trauma and to only begin to explore this at a time that is right for them.

It is within this stage of the process that we might start to introduce the concept of "traumatised personality." Although we do not explicitly use the term in a diagnostic manner, we can begin to bring psychoeducation into our interactions by helping people understand how early adversity and disorganised attachment processes impact on our psychological and physical development and how coping behaviours are designed to keep us safe, though often unconsciously.

The last few years have shown that much of the support we offer oscillates between Pretreatment stages 1-2, initially with an absence of any shared common language; keeping it simple whilst being genuinely interested and empathic is the most effective approach. As service use involvement may be neither linear nor constant, building rapport and trust via practicable and /or emotional support [attending appointments/ making telephone calls/filling out form/giving lifts/buying coffee] can scaffold the beginnings of a healing relationship.

We can then carefully and gradually begin to move sessions more towards conversations about change and how life might be different. As the relationship strengthens, and the individual begins to feel safer both with us and more generally in their environments and start to understand their own locus of control, we might start to introduce conversations about what they want to achieve through our work and how we (and others) can support them in this.

Stage 3—Contracting

Once initial trust is developed, and we have understood some of the early challenges of building engagement and enabling extreme levels of distress to decrease, we are able to sit alongside the individual as they tell their story. We found that by bearing witness to the story, supporting them to organise the story as a narrative and giving space for emotions and other processes to be validated and normalised, trauma-related coping strategies began to increase (Elbert, Schauer, & Neuner, 2022). For the mental health practitioner, this is also an opportunity to develop a more in-depth assessment of the person, which would have been impossible earlier in the work.

By this stage, we may have achieved significant goals, such as establishing the firm foundations of a trusting relationship, having a clear sense of a shared language, understanding the barriers to engagement with others, and the beginnings of discussions of achievable goals. Often the process of moving from first contact through to stage 3 might take several months or even years; we may have supported the person through many life changes (perhaps even into long-term accommodation) and may begin conversations about transitioning to work with other teams to meet more long-term goals such as trauma processing, recovery, or even vocational support.

It is worth acknowledging that, often, after some initial improvements and increased stability in their life, (from prison/street homelessness/psychiatric unit/homeless hostel into supported or independent living) people can (consciously or otherwise) withdraw, and that many people can feel more comfortable oscillating between periods of more intense involvement as, if built securely, our positive relationship endures and can be relighted at any time. For example, we met Brian less frequently once he moved into long-term, stable housing, and his "erratic" and "agitated" behaviour reduced significantly when he had his own front door.

In the initial stages, we certainly were present to support the individual to achieve goals, perhaps taking more of a role in the practical side, and often demonstrating our care by taking a lot of the responsibility. In stage 3, we would expect more clarity about roles and who is responsible for tasks, and supported the client to develop self-efficacy in addressing day-to-day issues, and problem-solving by themselves.

As barriers to trust come down and are replaced by hope, we can bring in other professionals to achieve goals. These conversations might involve referrals for assessments or investigations that might previously have been impossible, such as learning disability or cognitive impairment. There might be ongoing work with the team psychologist, developing a thorough psychological formulation, learning coping strategies and talking about endings.

Stage 4—Action

This is often a period of steady progress, increased independence, and the beginning of the final phase of our work. We notice that people feel less reliant on us and have started to improve their social networks. They have much more supportive relationships with professionals across the city and are more easily able to navigate conflict and difficulty when it arises. If insurmountable difficulty arises, by this stage people are often able to contact us for support without the situation leading to a crisis point.

Our role in stage 4 is to continue to function as a secure base for the individual whilst longer term goals are met. Other professionals are now on board, but we act as coordinators for the provision of care, continue to provide an emotional safe space, listen empathically, and reinforce new coping strategies, while constantly highlighting the progress that has been made.

This stage can be daunting and anxiety-provoking for all involved due to an understanding that we will eventually have to exit, but it is difficult to open conversations about it or acknowledge that a professional has taken a meaningful role in their lives. We work hard to open discussions and explore the relationship in our sessions, focusing on the progress they have made allowing a new person into their lives and the adaptations to new ways of relating.

Stage 5—Maintenance and Endings

In this stage, the process of bringing relationships to a close is the focus as we support transitions to new staff and services. Whereas in stage 4 we were introducing the prospect of endings, by this point we are beginning to confront very real issues of loss and grief. The process of developing a relationship with a mental health professional who is consistent and validating can be difficult in and of itself, and the prospect of losing the relationship can be painful.

Although the person may have started to develop positive relationships with new providers, the ending of this important relationship can be challenging for all involved. Revisiting and revising the role of new teams and new workers is important to ensure that people are aware that they have had control in their recovery. There remain very understandable fears and anxieties that new workers won't be able to achieve the same level of equality in the relationship, so it is important to guide the understanding of both self-efficacy and personal responsibility.

If goals have been achieved and the relationship continues to be supportive and equal, Stage 5 should also be a period of reflection and review. We try to balance the focus on processing the difficult emotions of endings alongside reviewing the progress made, and this can be an opportunity to highlight achievements—for example, a sustained period of accommodation stability, a reduction or abstinence from alcohol, or reestablished family relationships. It might also be a time to reinforce adaptive coping strategies, such as the ability to cope with anger more effectively, understanding anxiety in the context of threatening situations, or being able to simply spend time alone without feeling afraid. A level of appropriate self-disclosure is crucial here—people need to feel a sense of equality and hear that they have meant something to us.

When not working one to one with someone, being present and actively involved at various city-wide drop-ins and outreach activities can maintain (and improve) such relationships. Hull is not a large city, nor is it transitory in nature, so often we continue to meet and mix with people whom we have previously worked with and may well do so again.

Case Studies

Gary

Gary (21) was referred for mental health support by a housing association after a long period of being street homeless. They expressed concerns that he was talking about distressing things including demonic possession and was struggling/demotivated to manage the everyday aspects of life in his new apartment.

Gary presented as flat, and other than sit in his apartment in the dark all-day, he used to try to deal with his persecutions by taking drugs, in turn becoming less communicative and demotivated to attend to any of his daily needs. Being proactive, Gary's support worker spoke with the team psychologist [Dan] to see if he could offer some support.

Although initially suspicious and reluctant, Gary and Dan soon built up a strong, trusting bond and Dan was able to ascertain that Gary had been victim to multiple incidents of childhood abuse, neglect, and abandonment, which continued to drive Gary's fears over making any form of relationship.

After a period of support produced some much-needed safety and positivity for Gary, I [Chris] then began to work with him to offer some longer-term support, usually in the form of cups of coffee and walks in a local park. At the start, all was well as both Gary and I reflected on the work he'd done with Dan, but then…long periods of silence interspersed with conversations firmly fixed on Gary's religiosity. These were tough words to hear, so I can only imagine how hard it was for Gary to say them out loud.

I listened, answered, and offered my thoughts and opinions when appropriate, but I began to feel as though I was not doing anything for Gary. I often came back to the office after our meetings with him and felt like I wasn't doing anything, like I wasn't moving his recovery forward.

After a reflective team discussion on Psychologically Informed Environments one afternoon, I thought I may be putting too much emphasis on "doing" with Gary. I know this sounds far-fetched, but that same afternoon I texted Gary to arrange our next meeting and he replied by explaining how much he values our time together and thanking me for what I'd been doing and "not pushing it."

Thanks Gary—without realising it, you reminded me of the power of a positive relationship as the intervention, for me not to underestimate how spending time with someone can provide something worthwhile—an anchor, a focus, a release— which I still clearly need to be reminded of from time to time.

Ben

Ben (47) has had an adult life punctuated by prison, street homelessness, and other forms of precarious housing. When he was last released from prison to the streets, he returned to Hull to find himself banned from all hostels due to a reputation of aggressive behaviour toward other people and himself—his increased expression of suicidality was how he revealed his frustrations and anger at the world.

After a month or so of rough sleeping, Ben was arrested, and detained by police via the s.136 of the Mental Health Act. Fortunately, involved professionals (including Dan, me, Ben's probation officer, and pastor) were able to secure his safe release to a room at a local hostel with the hopefully watertight stipulation from the provider that a plethora of service providers (mental health, physical health, police, probation, adult social care, substance use) agreed to provide him with wrap-around support whilst living there.

So far, so good for the services, but Ben felt understandably overwhelmed, which led to him rejecting the chance to work with many of us. Due to previous work Ben had done with Dan, it surprisingly wasn't our Homeless Mental Health Team that he told to "go away."

Over the next few months filled with set meeting times, flexible meeting times, breakfasts, coffees, drives, and general common language construction, especially about sportswear and trainers, Ben and I developed a sound working relationship, albeit one which he couldn't always tolerate. But these almost six months spent in a single place was the longest Ben had ever done as an adult (outside of prison).

Unfortunately, Ben's mental health crises continued, but he almost always asked to speak with me even when talking to the local Crisis Team, although I didn't work there. If I could, I did. This was often possible because I worked in the neighbouring office.

Likewise, when Ben was brought in on a Section 136[26] again, I tried to ensure I was part of the ensuing Mental Health Act (1983) assessment with the AMHP and psychiatrists to offer Ben advocacy and the profes-

---

[26] Section 136 is part of the Mental Health Act in the United Kingdom that gives the police the powers to convey a person to a "place of safety" (hospital or mental health unit) if they present with symptoms of severe mental health distress

sionals some much-needed context. This happened more than once and seemed to provide Ben some soothing, which led to more effective outcomes being offered.

Martin

Martin (45) was another man who had been in and out of prison for most of his adult life and was a prolific polydrug user. After spending some time at the Winter Bed Provision, he moved into his own flat—his first in over twenty years.

After some time spent getting used to his flat (mainly partying) and not seeing me, Martin and I randomly met in the city centre one day at a local breakfast club. Remembering me from the Provision, he chatted with me, and I explained that I'd been coming to see him, but it never seemed the right time. So, I asked if now was? He agreed and we went for a coffee.

A pattern soon emerged of us meeting up, either at his flat or in a coffee shop/pub/pool hall, where we would speak at length about sports and mutually known areas of Hull and associates.

Whilst Martin's mental wellbeing was always a top priority for us both, we rarely spoke outside the above frames of reference. After we snaked back to his flat after playing billiards, during which he'd graciously let me win a couple of games, Martin casually turned his head and said, "I'm alright, you know…you're in my circle…I'd tell you if I wasn't."

And more times than not, he did. Even after one momentous time he didn't/couldn't, ended with him returning to prison, me then visiting him inside seemed to mean a lot to him.

Summary, and the Future of Pretreatment

Making, maintaining, improving, and positively ending relationships with people who remain, in a socio-political context, the most labelled, marginalised, and stigmatised, can be difficult. Working this way with people, being available and present, is both emotionally demanding and time-consuming, and, as such, it cannot be done in isolation. City-wide support from other agencies remains crucial and, in turn, the more that all practitioners can develop a greater understanding of Pretreatment, the more we can offer homeless people better continuity, coherence, and clarity.

The Homeless Mental Health Team is growing—we're recruiting at least another two practitioners, and this can be seen as evidence of the realisation of the team's Pretreatment work with people suffering from homelessness in Hull. This will provide an immediate opportunity to spend time with other involved agencies (including working with young people leaving the care system), getting to know them better, and introducing/maintaining/further developing Pretreatment across the city.

Furthermore, after discussion with other Pretreatment practitioners and psychologists, the HMHT in Hull is exploring the possibility of offering Single Session Therapy (SST) to people suffering from homelessness. Importantly, these preliminary discussions highlighted that SST, rather than being contradictory, can be complimentary to Pretreatment, so long as the intended outcomes remain realistic, i.e., building trust, rapport, and hope with people.

Longer-term, an obvious development area for our team and city is to improve the levels of co-production in service delivery (currently in its infancy) with service users who have worked with us previously (something we can learn more from our colleagues in substance use services). The NHS Trust within which we work have already proactively sought people's voices to share their experiences with trust board members, either directly in meetings or pre-recorded video, but this should only be the beginning. Integrating experts-by-experience within our team to offer people better, more attuned support is the goal. As ReNew (the substance use agency in Hull) has shown, it can be done to great effect.

We are fortunate to be well connected to the homeless mental health professional community across the UK, and the passion for supporting homeless people amongst the practitioners we have met is staggering. In the conversations and forums we have been part of so far, Pre-treatment therapy and the many varied and creative ways it can be delivered in services is always a central topic. It certainly is an exciting time in the development and implementation of Pre-treatment Therapy. In the next chapter, John Conolly speaks to the evolution and future possibilities of Pretreatment and Pre-treatment Therapy throughout the UK.

References

Bateman, A., & Fonagy, P. (2010). Mentalization based treatment for borderline personality disorder. *World Psychiatry, 9,* 11 – 15.

Bateman, A, & Fonagy, P. (2016). *Mentalization-based treatment of personality disorders: A practical guide.* Oxford, UK: Oxford University Press.

Bateman, A, & Fonagy, P. (2019). *Handbook of mentalization in mental health practice.* Washington, DC: American Psychiatric Publishing.

Bateman, A., Rüfenacht, E., Perroud, N., Debbané, M., Nolte, T., Shaverin, L., & Fonagy, P. (2023). Childhood maltreatment, dissociation and borderline personality disorder: Preliminary data on the mediational role of mentalizing in complex post-traumatic stress disorder. *Psychology and Psychotherapy: Theory, Research and Practice,* 2023; 00, 1 – 17.

Bryant, R. A. (2019). Post-traumatic stress disorder: A state-of-the-art review of evidence and challenges. *World Psychiatry,* 18, 259 – 269.

Courtois, C. A. (2008). Complex trauma, complex reactions: Assessment and treatment. *Psychological Trauma: Theory, Research, Practice, & Policy,* Vol S, 1, 86 – 100.

Courtois, C. A., & Ford, J. D. (2012). *Treatment of complex trauma: A sequenced, relationship-based approach.* New York, NY: Guilford Press.

Dowson, C. (2022). *Hull homeless mental health team: Towards emergent models of healing in homelessness.* Accessed 2nd Mar 2024 from https://tinyurl.com/hullhome

Fonagy, P., & Allison, E. (2014). The role of mentalizing and epistemic trust in the therapeutic relationship. *Psychotherapy, 51*(3), 372-380.

Fonagy, P., Luyten, P., Allison, E., & Campbell, C. (2021). What we have changed our minds about: Part 2. Borderline personality disorder, epistemic trust and the developmental significance of social communication. *Borderline Personality Disorder and Emotion Dysregulation, 4*(9).

Herman, J. L. (1992). *Trauma and recovery.* New York, NY: Basic Books.

Herman, J. L. (1998). Recovery from psychological trauma. *Psychiatry and Clinical Neuroscience, 52*(Suppl. 1), S98 – S103.

Hertzberg, D., & Boobis, S. (2022). *The unhealthy state of homelessness 2022: Findings from the homeless health needs audit.* https://tinyurl.com/homelink2

Irving, A., & Harding, J. (2022). *The prevalence of trauma among people who have experienced homelessness in England.* Oasis Community Housing. https://tinyurl.com/oasis2home

Keats, H., Maguire, N., Johnson, R., & Cockersell, P. (2012). *Psychologically informed services for homeless people: Good practice guide.* Department of Communities and Local Government. https://tinyurl.com/keatsh

Larkin, P. (1974). *High Windows.* London: Faber & Faber.

Levy, J. S. (2000). Homeless outreach: On the road to pretreatment alternatives. *Families in Society: The Journal of Contemporary Social Services, 81*(4), 360 – 368.

Levy, J. S. (2021). *Pretreatment in Action: Interactive exploration from homeless to housing stabilization.* Ann Arbor, MI: Loving Healing Press.

Maercker, A., Brewin, C. R., Bryant, R. A., Cloitre, M., van Ommeren, M., Jones, L. M., Humayan, A., Kagee, A., Llosa, A. E., Rousseau, C., Somasundaram, D. J., Souza, R., Suzuki, Y., Weissbecker, I., Wessely, S. C., First, M. B., & Reed, G. M. (2013). Diagnosis and classification of disorders specifically associated with stress: Proposals for ICD-11. *World Psychiatry*, 12(3), 198-206.

Norcross, J. C., Krebs, P. M., & Prochaska, J. O. (2011). Stages of change. *Journal of Clinical Psychology, 67*(2), 143 – 154.

Prochaska, J. O., & DiClemente, C. C. (1983). Stages and processes of self-change of smoking: Toward an integrated model of change. *Journal of Consulting and Clinical Psychology, 51*(3), 390 – 395.

Rees, S. (2009). *Mental ill health in the adult single homeless population*. London: Crisis UK.

Theodorou, N., Johnsen, S., Watts, B., & Burley, A. (2021). Improving multiple exclusion homelessness (MEH) services: frontline worker responses to insecure attachment styles. *The Journal of Mental Health Training, Education and Practice, 16*(6), 421-432.

Life in Hull Corresponding Data Sources:

Crime Rate-website, (Updated June, 10 2024). https://crimerate.co.uk/east-riding-of-yorkshire/kingston-upon-hull

Guardian-website, (July, 2013). https://www.theguardian.com/uk-news/the-northerner/2013/jul/19/top-10-myths-about-hull

Hull City Council Report, (September, 2019). https://data.hull.gov.uk/wp-content/uploads/Briefing-Report-Hull-English-Indices-of-Deprivation-2019.pdf

Hull City Council: Hull's JSNA, (March, 2024). https://www.hulljsna.com/adults/lifestyle-factors-adults/drugs-adults/

Hull Live-website, (February, 2023). https://www.hulldailymail.co.uk/news/uk-world-news/crime-map-ranks-most-dangerous-8191037

Hull Live-website, (December, 2023). https://www.hulldailymail.co.uk/news/hull-east-yorkshire-news/crime-rising-humber-police-well-8967668

UK Parliament: House of Commons Library, (March, 2024). https://commonslibrary.parliament.uk/research-briefings/sn06988/

Varbes-website, (Accessed July, 21 2024). https://www.varbes.com/crime/kingston-upon-hull-city-of-crime

8 Time for a Paradigm change? Pretreatment and Pre-treatment Therapy for People experiencing Homelessness in the UK

John Conolly

We ask for no statistics of the killed,
For nothing political impinges on
This single casualty, or all those gone,
Missing or healing, sinking or dispersed,
Hundreds of thousands counted, millions lost.

More than an accident and less than willed,
Is every fall, and this one like the rest.
However, others calculate the cost,
To us the final aggregate is one,
One with a name, one transferred to the blest.
And though another stoops and takes the gun,
We cannot add the second to the first.

Karl Shapiro, *Elegy for a Dead Soldier* (1998)

Introduction

In Great Britain, the predominant paradigm of psychological and mental health treatment as delivered by the NHS (the National Health Service), to people who are without a home is the Medical Model, which bases itself solely on quantitative evidence. Contrary to the above, does indeed, assume that "the second [can be added] to the first," something of course simply impossible at the level of personal experience and meaning. Pretreatment, however, focuses in at the individual level of meaning, and by so doing can come to understand someone's "Psychic Home" (the mental representation of their home of origin, with its relationship and identification patterns) and thereby develop the knowledge of the support needed to ensure sustainable rehousing, and ideally homemaking for that person. What follows is a review of the evolving practice of Pre-treatment Therapy for people without homes in the UK.

Paradigms

In *The Structure of Scientific Revolutions* (1967), Thomas Kuhn coined the term, "Paradigm," to describe how a scientific community comes to agree on a particular model with which to solve a problem and guide future research, which occurs in a period of "normal science."

When the old model, however, no longer satisfactorily explains new problems, this ushers in a period of revolutionary science or "Paradigm shift," when a new model replaces the old one. Pretreatment, as Matt suggests (see Chapter 2), and as I have come to believe, could potentially represent such a Paradigm shift for the care and support of people experiencing homelessness.

Paradigms are perspectives of the world that explain things so differently that they cannot co-exist. Ultimately, the choice of a paradigm depends on personal choice by scholars and practitioners' personalities and preferences that underlies the adoption of which paradigm will be chosen (Hendersen & Tendler, 2017).

Becoming homeless and living in a condition of homelessness is a complex and traumatic experience. As a psychological therapies practitioner myself and leader of a small National Health Service (NHS)[27] counselling service in London, I came to realize that mainstream psychological approaches fail to credit this. Therefore, unfortunately it is extremely difficult if not impossible for homeless people to access, engage with and derive the potential benefits of mainstream psychological approaches.

The concept of "continuum of harm" (Johns et al., 2021) captures this well in that it draws attention to how the everyday language or stereotyping used by professionals in institutional settings can amplify

---

[27] The NHS is the publicly funded national healthcare system in the UK and provides a comprehensive service, available to all irrespective of gender, race, disability, age, sexual orientation, religion, or belief.

and reproduce the effects of marginalisation and trauma and elicit reactions that further exclude and punish.

Thus, the following vignette is drawn from the first essay in the anthology, *The knot: An essay collection on the interconnectedness of poverty, trauma, and multiple disadvantage* (Johns, et al., 2021, p10)

Everyday encounter #1: Sally

Sally, a 35-year-old mother of five, attends her first appointment at the local health centre to develop a mental health care plan. Sally is accompanied by her community support worker, Helen.

The doctor greets them both, invites them to sit down and asks Sally what has brought her to see him.

Doctor: Good afternoon, I'm Dr Smith. How can I help you today?

Sally: [announces loudly] I'm f....d in the head!

Doctor: Excuse me, Ms... we don't tolerate any abusive behaviour in this clinic. I'm sorry, we'll have to end this appointment.

Helen: Are you kidding, doctor? She wasn't abusing anyone—she was just describing her state of mind!

Doctor: I'm sorry. We have a zero-tolerance policy. If you don't leave now, I'll have to call security.

Sally: It's OK Helen, my bad! Let's go...

A different response from Dr Smith could have had such a different effect, potentially quite a life changing one:

Sally: "I'm f....d in the head!"

Doctor: "Yes, I'm sure it does feel like that sometimes or even quite often. Can you tell me more about it...?

Sally: "Well, it's like this ..."

Pretreatment and Pre-treatment Therapy

Pretreatment on the other hand puts the whole process of engagement under the microscope, delineating its different phases, and the most useful ways of supporting and influencing each one through the development of a common language between the worker and the person in need.

Jay developed Pretreatment from his experience of doing outreach work, contacting people, and engaging people on the streets, and supporting them in accessing local community resources.

Pre-treatment Therapy also pays particular attention to language, both verbal and nonverbal, (including the use of and positioning of oneself in physical space, i.e., "territory"), and presupposes that people usually have the potential to change if given appropriate attention and care. They can move on, and increasingly live out their potential, if offered a compassionate, supportive, empowering relationship.

Pretreatment and Pre-treatment Therapy, with its focus on "Relationship," asks, "What is MY responsibility in this person's reaction right now? What and how have I said, not said, done, not done something that could have led to this person closing, storming out, shouting at me? Did I move too suddenly? Did I allow a judgemental tone to creep into my voice? Was something in ME triggered?"

For example, did Dr Smith above feel moral outrage at a young mother speaking that way—did it touch a whole host of assumptions regarding the ideal of "mothering?" Did it lead him to an overzealous interpretation of policy? Was he newly in the role and felt the need to prove himself? Did any of these things shift his focus of attention from the person in front of him needing his help, to himself and his need to protect his (ideal) self-image?

In other words, Pre-treatment Therapy requires the practitioner to be sufficiently confident and self-aware to have the ability to suspend their judgement, put their own needs on hold, regulate their emotions, demonstrate compassion toward other people's difficulties, and have the life experience to know that there are always reasons for someone's misfortune, and their being overwhelmed. In other words, ultimately people have the ability to put themselves and their preconceptions into question. No easy task for anyone!

The Westminster Homeless Health Counselling Service

This is buildings based, and the counsellors are in community day and medical centres where homeless people can come to meet their immediate basic needs, or medical needs. However, as NHS employees, we are subject to practicing within NHS norms of practice, which are still based on the "medical model" of diagnosis and treatment. NHS psychological treatments are (predominantly) time-limited and targeted to achieve predetermined outcomes in symptom reduction as defined by professionals and evidence-based medicine. This is epitomized by the National Institute for Health and Care Excellence (NICE), which produces guidance for health and social care practitioners based on the rigorous, independent assessment of complex evidence. This usually consists of Randomised Controlled Trials.

For example, due to the sheer volume of evidence, Cognitive Behaviour Therapy (CBT)[28] is one of the most recommended modes of psychological interventions for people, whether it is evidenced for a particular population or not. The weight of evidence regarding its effectiveness for the mainstream population seems to lead to the assumption that it is effective across the board, despite it being especially helpful regarding a single current issue rather than several complex chronic ones.

So, people who are homeless are routinely "treated" using methods like CBT, which is mainly evidenced on populations with the fundamental security and stability of a home. Thus, the evidence base here simply does not apply well to a homeless population.

As Rosemary Cameron points out: "Public institutions such as the police, and the mental health professions, operate within larger systems of ideals and ideas." (Cameron, 2020, p. 122).

The Medical Model

This is based on deductive reasoning, whereby theory is used to diagnose a specific "case," and its "treatment." Pretreatment on the other hand uses inductive thinking whereby through careful observation of the person an attempt is made to understand that person in all of their complexity, and uniqueness. We accomplish this by building together a trusting relationship and a common language. This provides us with a greater understanding of how our clients view and experience the world. Only then can we begin to develop a working hypothesis, from which to

[28] Cognitive behavioural therapy (CBT) is a talking therapy that can help manage psychological problems by changing the way people think and behave. It's most commonly used to treat anxiety and depression, but can be useful for other mental and physical health problems. CBT deals with a current problem, rather than focusing on issues from the past.

eventually theorize, and generalize. The first assumes that all is known about a population; the second (Pretreatment) that on the contrary, little is known but much needs to be learnt about a population before any theories and interventions can be developed and effectively applied.

We could have a possible instance of institutional and systemic exclusion here, in that it seems to be assumed that homeless people are simply those who lack accommodation and should therefore be cared for like anyone else, but for the added provision of accommodation or at least shelter (however temporary). Or they are perceived as mentally ill and therefore to be treated by mental health services, which (in the UK) do not perceive trauma, even chronic, complex trauma as a mental illness. Finally, homeless people may be seen as "non-deserving" in that they have "chosen" their lifestyle, or they are a "criminal element" due to their addictions with the reasons for these choices and afflictions never being considered.

It will be seen how Pre-treatment Therapy, with its non-time limited support, allows for a much deeper and nuanced understanding of homelessness, and therefore the devising and application of more sustainable solutions to it.

In mainstream NHS services, no consideration is given to contextual factors that cause and maintain symptoms, or how they are interpreted. Also, no account is taken of individual idiosyncrasies in the expression of distress and suffering, or that similar symptoms may have different meanings and different causes or result from different maintaining factors.

Thus, while symptomatic improvement may well occur after a cognitive behaviour therapy (CBT) programme on say, the management of anxiety or depression, these symptoms will unfortunately reappear after a while, once the person returns to their original triggering environment, or the effects of the compassionate attention they received from their CBT therapist wear off after the termination of the programme.

This can happen even when someone is "housed" in accommodation, and the suitability of the accommodation is not considered, nor the factors preceding their homelessness.

Thus, I have supported people recovering from addiction who were placed in hostels together with people with active addictions. A young woman, Suzanne, was placed in an establishment with a history of sexual harassment complaints, and unfortunately, she was severely harassed and fell into a co-dependent relationship. Others have been suffering from chronic depression or Persistent depressive disorder[29] (in one case for some twenty years), and once accommodated in their own flat were expected to somehow find the means of connecting with the local community. This is unlikely, and therefore unsafe or even dangerous. The transitional support offered was simply unable to cater for such entrenched depression (and inability to reach out and connect). The same applies to people suffering from avoidant personality disorder[30], which can often underlie such chronic and enduring depression.

Pre-treatment Therapy, with its emphasis on connection and attachment, time, and common language development, allows for a detailed understanding to emerge, and therefore the provision of timely, appropriate, and calibrated support. This includes extensive transition management, and, crucially, post transition settlement support from the same familiar and trusted counsellor/psychotherapist. Thus, I have supported Jacob, an elderly man with "avoidant personality disorder" over a period of seven years, two suicide attempts and three rehousing cycles (his story will be returned to further down).

The public tends to assume that homeless people with mental health needs can be supported to access the local community mental health services. However, as already mentioned, these services do not usually have the depth of experience and understanding regarding the psychology of social exclusion and the continuum of harm dynamics they inadvertently set up via prolonged and intrusive assessment interviews. Without a trusting relationship in place, these interactions retraumatise people and add to their history of "toxic help" (Conolly, 2018).

---

[29] Persistent depressive disorder is a continuous, long-term form of depression, https://www.mayoclinic.org/diseases-conditions/persistent-depressive-disorder - accessed 16 Feb 2024

[30] People with avoidant personality disorder have chronic feelings of inadequacy and are highly sensitive to being negatively judged by others. Though they would like to interact with others, they tend to avoid social interaction due to the intense fear of being rejected by others. Hence the very high risk of depression and even deliberate self-harm.

Thus, I have often supported people at the stage where we both thought they would be ready to engage with mental health services. I have even briefed these services regarding possible triggers, and what strategies to implement if they are activated. Predictably, these very same individuals come back to me in an even more hopeless state of distress and adamant that they would never again engage with the mental health system. This is what I have termed the affliction of toxic help in my previous writings on Pre-treatment Therapy. We have found Pretreatment to be a helpful guide for clinicians who work with highly vulnerable people.

Unfortunately, mental health services are also very much oversubscribed, which has led them to raise the bar regarding the acceptance of referrals. Thus, even specialist community mental health services for homeless people will not consider personality disorder, or what I refer to as "traumatised personality" (Conolly, 2018), despite its devastating impact and its high prevalence amongst homeless people. Furthermore, the rare personality disorder treatment services available in the community will only accept the two most common types, emotionally unstable (borderline personality disorder) and anti-social, out of the ten subtypes classified in the DSM V American Psychiatric Diagnostic and Statistical Manual (2023). Thus sadly, waiting times for community mental health services can be eighteen months to two years in some cases, and many homeless people suffering with traumatised personalities (or personality disorder), especially of the avoidant type, will not have access to any specialist treatment at all.

Why Pre-treatment Therapy?

In short, we are here for unhoused people, whose main priority is simple survival. When referred, if they turn up, it will probably be with chemically-induced and trauma-induced states of consciousness (such as dissociation for example), mental health driven concerns, lack of insight and orientation in time and space (psychosis, drug induced or not), sleep deprivation, hunger, cold, and histories of "toxic help:" failed engagements, abuse, and betrayals (Conolly, 2018a; 2018b).

Mainstream counselling and psychotherapy services will reject these people on the grounds of inability to attend regular appointments at specific times, being emotionally unregulated and aggressive well beyond waiting room norms, and unable to manage their addiction(s).

The term Pre-treatment Therapy was chosen for two reasons:

To denote the extent of therapeutic knowledge and practice necessary to have the confidence and skills to go beyond mainstream theories and trainings, so one can engage and maintain that engagement with unhoused people, in an NHS buildings-based environment.

To create a bridging language between two very different paradigms. One is "Pretreatment" and its self-questioning stance of interested, compassionate curiosity and its non-time limited way of working; the other the culture of the National Health Service (NHS)—a gigantic health service of national proportions, based on "evidence-based medicine."

Pretreatment was invaluable in providing a model of understanding regarding the engagement and supporting of homeless people, but how to promote this in an evidence-based environment of practice?

I decided to raise the profile of the counselling service and the Pretreatment approaches by going public, speaking at conferences, and to offer skills-based training packages.

Conference Presentations

I presented at the Royal College of Psychiatry on the topic of "How to Engage People who are Homeless" (Conolly, 2022). I made it clear that Pre-treatment Therapy was based on pre-existing (related) models of well-evidenced knowledge and practice:

Pretreatment

- Levy (2010, 2013, 2018, 2021)
- Stages of Change, (Prochaska & Norcross 2003)
- Common Language development (see Levy)
- Motivational Interviewing (Miller & Rollnick, 2012, Wagner & Ingersol, 2012).
- Trauma-Informed Care Principles, (SAMHSA, 2014)
- Trauma recovery stages (Herman 2015)

- Safety (emotional regulation and stabilization of circumstances)
- Remembering & Grieving
- Restoring Relationships

Attachment Theory

- Secure Base (Bowlby,1975,1982a,1982b,2005, Holmes, 2006, 2018)
- Mentalization (Bateman & Fonagy, 2004, 2006, 2012, 2016)

Pre-treatment Therapy was thus born out of a clinical need, as well as an organisational one, to justify what the service needed to provide:

- Ongoing open-ended support to avoid potentially life-threatening crises in the face of recurring triggering encounters with other services and life events
- Internal psychological change in the adoption of new coping strategies
- The facilitation of finding new meaning(s) in life
- The recognition of mental health issues such as Persistent Depression Disorder and Avoidant Personality Disorder
- The support for reconnections with past relationships or reaching out for new ones

The original aims of the counselling service had been to relieve immediate psychological distress and reactivate basic coping resources, but we very quickly discovered that basic coping resources were in the main lacking and had to be painstakingly built up over (sometimes) many years. We also found that in the face of long mental health service waiting lists and continuum of harm dynamics, we not only had to help people relieve and manage their symptoms, but also unlearn their habitual destructive coping strategies and replace them with more adapted ones. Thus, by default, we found ourselves in the position of having to facilitate deep internal psychological change in people (i.e., therapy and not exclusively the provision of an enhanced engagement process).

Skills-based Training

Due to demand from frontline services and support from Pathway (UK's leading homeless healthcare charity, which helps the NHS to create hospital teams to support homeless patients, and trains professionals across the country), I began to develop the following trauma-informed skills-based training package:

- Social Exclusion and Trauma: "The Continuum of Harm"
- Vicarious Trauma and the Supportive Organisation
- Trauma-Informed Listening Skills—Making Someone Feel Understood
- Trauma-Informed Motivational Interviewing Skills—Agenda Co-production
- Trauma-Informed Self-Assertion Skills—Setting boundaries
- Staff Support and Discussion Groups—Self-Reflective Skills

NHS England (the strategic arm of the NHS for England) invited me to deliver the fifth module on setting boundaries to one of their services and subsequently streamed my delivery of the module on their national online platform.

Pretreatment and Pre-treatment Therapy Developments

Pretreatment and Pre-treatment Therapy presently seem to be attracting increasing attention both from frontline practitioners, in that it speaks to their experience in a way that makes sense to them, and from the Commissioners of mental health services for people without homes. This includes the Humber Teaching NHS Foundation Trust, the South East Essex Community Psychological Services, and the Leeds & York Partnership Foundation Trust, which have all recommended Pretreatment and Pre-treatment Therapy as models of intervention.

However, apart from Psychiatry, Psychology is the main profession regarding mental health and psychological therapies in the NHS, and it is to these professions that commissioners invariably turn to in the implementation and delivery of these new services. These professions base their practice and interventions on evidence-based techniques then find themselves at quite a loss when faced with the complexity, severity and chronicity of homeless people's symptoms and suffering.

Thus, the lead clinician of one of the above services, an experienced clinical psychologist, contacted me directly for advice and support re the delivery of Pretreatment and Pre-treatment Therapy. In fact, he co-authored the prior chapter—Dan Southall.

Two to three years ago, the UK government funded a national network of mental health services for homeless people and Dan quickly recognized the need for more readily available and pertinent guidance. He therefore set up a national online support network, The "setting up services forum," which now boasts some eighty plus members and to which I am happy to advise. A very recent development has been the establishment of a separate working group to develop evidence and outcome measures specifically for people who are homeless.

My own NHS trust's Central London Community Healthcare Homeless Health Service, as well as the Specialist Weight Management Service, and the Pathway Faculty for Homeless and Inclusion Health have also endorsed Pretreatment and Pre-treatment Therapy. I was also invited to join the standing committee of a research project by St. James Hospital and Trinity College, Dublin, on Trauma Informed Communication Skills training for hospital staff, as well as the standing committee for a new mental health service for homeless people in Dublin.

Limited Institutional Progress and the Need for Research

In March 2022, guidance on "Integrated health and social care for people experiencing homelessness" (NG214) was published by the National Institute for Health and Care Excellence (NICE), an executive non-departmental public body, sponsored by the British Department of Health and Social Care.

Some of the main points in the guideline include the recognition that:

- Homelessness and poor health are intertwined.
- People experiencing homelessness and rough sleeping require more targeted approaches to make health and social care more accessible, (flexible appointment times, "one stop shops" for multiple services).

- Care should be empathetic, trauma-informed and person-centred ("longer contact times in developing and sustaining trusting relationships").
- Joint commissioning should be the norm for health and social care, housing, criminal justice, and domestic abuse.
- Multidisciplinary outreach care, including drug and alcohol and mental health workers, should be performed in non-traditional settings, such as on the street, hostels, or day centres.
- Services should be co-designed and co-delivered with people having experienced homelessness themselves.

Unusually, however, no guidance was included on how staff should implement these guidelines, especially on how to develop and sustain a trusting, person-centred, trauma-informed relationship. For instance, in the guideline on borderline personality disorder (CG78), dialectical behaviour therapy (DBT) and mentalization-based therapy (MBT) are specifically mentioned as the psychological therapy programmes of choice for inpatient treatment. In addition, cognitive analytic therapy (CAT), cognitive behavioural therapy (CBT), schema-focused therapy (SFT), and transference focused therapy (TFT), were mentioned for Outpatient Psychosocial interventions. (NICE, guideline [CG78], 2009).

I mention the "Integrated health and social care for people experiencing homelessness" guideline to illustrate how yet again it is mental health workers and psychologists who are turned to and assumed to have the core training to work with and support homeless people constructively and effectively. As I have already pointed out, unfortunately, in the main they do not.

Thus, although a significant step forward, this national guideline does not go far enough in that it fails to provide any guidance on the nature of the care and support that needs to be offered. Wouldn't it be wonderful if Pretreatment (Therapy) were to be recommended as the intervention of choice? However, this would need the careful and systematic building up of an evidence base NICE could consider.

In the hierarchy of studies for obtaining evidence, systematic reviews of randomised controlled trials (RCTs) are the most respected (regarding especially drug treatments), but are also the most complex to implement with non-drug interventions, and expensive to carry out.[31] The same applies with controlled observational cohort studies on the next level down the hierarchy of evidence, where a group, or cohort of people, is followed, up to several years after the intervention. This is notoriously difficult with homeless people.

Already it appears that evidence deemed to be the most credible cannot be readily gathered regarding homeless populations, due to a whole host of reasons (cost, complexity, practicalities), but not least an ignorance about the nature of the phenomenon itself.

Are we yet again rubbing up against an instance of institutional and systemic exclusion here, in that the very evidence required is simply not available practically and financially, as well as applicable for this population group?

Moving away from the giddy heights of RCTs, I will now turn to two vignettes that clearly illustrate the complexities of living without a home and why Pretreatment and Pre-treatment Therapy are so apt at dealing effectively with that phenomenon in all its complexity.

The Case of Suzanne

Suzanne was referred to me several years ago by the psychiatrist at the medical centre, wondering what I would make of her, since her expert opinion was that Suzanne was delusional. Suzanne's story when I heard it was certainly out of the ordinary, but in my opinion, it didn't imply that she was out of touch with reality. This was confirmed when I checked certain facts out.

She was a young woman of south Asian origins, claiming to be from an influential family from that part of the world and having claimed asylum here on the grounds of her life being in danger after having alienated them. Her application had been accepted, given her family's reputation and the nature of the culture. Defying her family's authority most certainly put her life at risk. A phone call to the relevant authorities confirmed this.

She had come to London after the completion of her degree, but knew no one, and had nowhere to go to. She found herself in a hostel for

[31] https://patient.info/doctor/different-levels-of-evidence - accessed the 2nd Sep 2023.

homeless people, which she found extremely distressing, for she had been accustomed to a certain lifestyle. She was also grieving the loss of ties with her family, and feeling adrift, as well as the memories of the emotional and physical abuse she had endured at their hands. She felt lonely, vulnerable, lost, and with no future. This led her to self-medicate with alcohol.

Initially, Suzanne would pop in at the walk-in clinics and there would be weeks sometimes even months when I wouldn't see her. It became all too clear that she could not tolerate being alone, and due to her looks was often the target of men's attentions.

After some months without any news from her, she suddenly appeared in a great state of distress and somewhat diminished physically. She had made friends at the hostel and after a bout of drinking had been sexually harassed. My work at that time was supporting her through the emotional roller coaster of the legal process and helping her manage her anxiety, and the re-experiencing of PTSD symptoms.

After that she disappeared for some months, until she again re-appeared in distress. Despite the above episode, she had made friends with some other young people at the hostel and had drifted into taking drugs with them. One evening she had collapsed from an overdose and had been found by someone who was very kind.

A relationship developed, but unfortunately the "kind" man turned out to be prone to fits of uncontrollable jealousy and even physical violence toward her. Against her better judgement, she was unable to break off the relationship. I explained about co-dependency (whereby relationship partners can be said to be addicted to each other) and the various possible means to break away from it, but to no avail.

I no longer heard anything from her again, until one day I received a call from a house outside of London, where she told me, she was being held as a virtual prisoner and she was desperate to come back to London. By phone I supported her on how best to get back.

However, the relationship resumed, and it became apparent that the man in question had a long history of violence and drug related crime, as well as a string of controlling relationships. She became addicted herself and my work then focused on helping her overcome that.

A further period of silence ensued until yet again she approached me to say that the assaults had become more frequent and violent until one day the police called by the neighbours had found her barely alive.

She at last broke off the relationship and I supported her through the psychological and emotional process. I also supported her through the process of rehousing into a one-bedroom flat and how to maintain it, while also thinking about her future and what kind of life she wanted.

I explained about the "traumatised personality" and supported her transition onto a specialist treatment programme. At last contact, she had completed the programme, was seeking employment, and was free of her ex-partner.

Points of Note

The first point of note is that despite numerous and prolonged absences, Suzanne had the courage, in the face of repeated self-perceived failures and self-blame, to nonetheless reach out to me multiple times. This I believe was due to the trust that Pretreatment's accepting, non-judgemental approach had enabled to develop. The focus on how Suzanne understood her experiences, the meaning she attributed to them, and working with these in a compassionate, accepting manner enabled this to happen. As we have seen with the continuum of harm, professsionals are all too prone to judge too quickly and without sufficient knowledge, just as with my psychiatrist colleague believing that Suzanne was delusional, due to her unusual origins.

A second point is that I supported Suzanne over a period of years, allowing for that trust to develop, but also for me to begin to piece together some of the possible underlying dynamics to the rollercoaster of crises she was experiencing over that period. Thus, it became apparent that due to her childhood abuse, she was in fact suffering from a "personality disorder," this driving her need for company at all costs, including falling into drugs and an abusive relationship. Had she approached a different service or clinician for each separate crisis, she would have been treated specifically for that crisis, not what was underlying it and all the others.

Third, I offered psychological and emotional support as and when needed.

Fourth, instead of focusing in on any symptom Suzanne presented with, I asked what her understanding of it was. What did she think it was about, what did it mean? Also, how did she think she could help herself with it, or what did she think prevented her from doing so? I made clear that this was a collaborative endeavour—I respected her experience and her knowledge of her strengths and weaknesses. I would also proffer information or share my view on things to ensure that her decisions were as informed as possible.

Fifth, I worked with whatever distress and its expression Suzanne presented with. I did not arbitrarily limit myself to a certain category of symptoms only, like depression, anxiety, addiction etc.

Finally, I also discussed and helped her process practical matters, like how to navigate the legal system or the housing system, etc.

The Case of Jacob

Jacob came to the medical centre while sleeping out on the streets, as his legs were hurting, and the doctor had suggested he have a chat with me. It was December some years ago, and it was cold. Given his elderly age, I suggested he consider emergency accommodation over the festive period, and he reluctantly agreed.

From there he was transferred to a hostel, which he hated. He threatened to leave several times. I was able to persuade him to remain. He was eventually transferred to a studio, which he didn't like mainly due to the caretakers of the building. I kept phone contact with him, encouraging him to connect with the local services there, which he steadfastly refused to do. After a year or so, he left the studio and disappeared.

I issued a national "vulnerable adult safeguard alert," not only due to his age, but also given his history of suicide attempts that had emerged piecemeal over the time I had been supporting him.

His father had had mental health issues and frequently moved the family during his childhood. As an adult, Jacob had had a series of administrative jobs, but had found himself to be the target of bullying, harassment, and intimidation from other colleagues, usually an older person in authority, driving him to keep on moving to other jobs. He was able to make the odd male friend at work, usually a younger colleague from another country, and with whom he would go out to the theatre or to the restaurant. These friendships ended, however, when these young men returned to their countries of origin. Although he was able to maintain living in a flat for several decades, he suffered from intense loneliness there and believes that he has been suffering from depression and insomnia throughout that timeframe. He remembered having attempted to take his own life several times over that period. He became homeless upon leaving his flat in the face of harassment from people he found frightening and intimidating.

A while after the "vulnerable adult safeguard alert" had gone out, someone contacted me to say that he believed that Jacob was at an emergency centre, which I rang explaining who I was. Jacob contacted me later and I resumed my support both face to face and by phone, depending on his whereabouts, as he moved around a lot, revisiting his old sleeping haunts on the streets.

Jacob eventually found a one-bedroom flat just before the Covid-19 pandemic and Lockdown. We kept contact via regular phone calls.

However, as before, he found the flat also unbearable. This was mainly due to some fractious relationships with some people in nominal authority managing the building there. As soon as lockdown was lifted, he paid his bills, let me know of his intention and handed in the keys. I made clear to him I thought this was very unwise. However, I ultimately respected the choices he made and continued to support him while on the streets (again)!

And this I did, even stored some of his belongings in my office, and ensured his access to the medical centre showers, all the time supporting him emotionally by giving him the space to process his intense and varied experiences on the street (mainly consisting of fear). I also aimed at helping him clarify his immediate, medium- and long-term needs, as well the decisions and actions he needed to take. With much emotional support he eventually agreed to move into yet another housing association studio flat, which although he continually threatened to leave for the first four months, he somehow managed to retain.

Points of Note

Again, the crucial factor here is trust. Jacob was open to accepting my support across his various circumstances. The first time he abandoned his studio flat, he gave me absolutely no indication of this and simply disappeared. However, he contacted me once he knew I had called the emergency shelter. The second time he abandoned his flat, he told me about his intent and was open to hearing (although not act on) my opinion regarding his choice. This trust enabled me to support him through two cycles of homelessness and re-housing and likely avoid the more nefarious consequences of such circumstances.

Most services would cease their support to Jacob once he was housed, and the resettling process would have to be restarted from scratch. The new workers involved having scant background information, and with very little initial trust in place, Jacob could again very easily take flight and disappear.

As with Suzanne, my prolonged support of Jacob enabled me to develop a working hypothesis of what might be his mental health support needs. Although he presents with chronic depression and insomnia, he is also a perfectionist, and holds on to a very rigid black and white view of right and wrong. He becomes extremely anxious when required to do a task in public, like filling in a form for example, and is also very distrustful of people and their motivations. All this results in his inability to make and sustain supportive relationships and he feels extremely lonely and vulnerable. This I believe is the profile of someone suffering from a variety of personality disorder traits, including Obsessive-Compulsive, Avoidant, and possibly Paranoid.[32]

This underscores how, by focusing on relationship, Pretreatment and Pre-treatment Therapy can access the underlying mental health states of people who are homeless. Something that has been named "The Psychic Home" developed within the actual physical home of the family of origin. This is the organising psychic structure of a person's identity, derived from the internalization of attachment style and family member identifications. (Kennedy, 2014)

"In the secure home, the parents provide continuity over time in their homemaking, providing a supportive base for the children to eventually leave, and ultimately to build up, their own home. A stable psychic home involves individuals being recognized as being autonomous yet

[32] https://www.verywellhealth.com/personality-disorders, accessed 30 Dec 2023.

dependent and receiving respect for their own individuality with secure attachments." (Kennedy, 2014, p 26)

As we know, this ideal is unfortunately subject to many challenges including Adverse Childhood Events (ACEs), grinding poverty, domestic violence, war and forced migration, trafficking, etc. This leaving many people who are chronically homeless with a somewhat impoverished psychic home, impacted by early trauma(s) of one kind or another and making it difficult for them to ever establish any sense of belonging, since they find it difficult to reach out and connect with people, and therefore feeling "at home" wherever they might be.

As we have seen, Jacob's predicament is his inability to establish and maintain supportive relationships, I believe because of his father having moved him so often when growing up. So, although he had been able to live in a flat for some twenty years, due to his isolation he felt unworthy of support, and he didn't consider it possible to confront the frightening people in his building and assert his rights, and so he fled onto the streets. Maybe he felt it was where he deserved to be and the only place where he belonged. It needs to be noted that he attempted to take his life several times while living there. He has repeated this pattern when confronted with any perceived/experienced challenging relationship. This suggests that Jacob needs some support in bolstering his "psychic home" and being taught social and self-assertion skills, as well as helped in developing a meaningful social network, to have any sense of belonging, of mattering to someone, and having any chance of transforming what would otherwise be temporary accommodation into a home where he could feel he belongs.

Way Forward

I have had the privilege of being allowed the space to deliver Pre-treatment Therapy in an NHS context and the reputation of the service has grown organically from the ground up. The staff at the day and medical centres for homeless people in Westminster have witnessed and experienced for themselves how the "hard to reach" patients or clients have been engaged and been able to transform their lives. Thus, the counselling service is experienced as a trusted and valuable resource. Furthermore, my manager has often commented how low staff sickness absence levels were, compared to other services. I am proud of how passionate the counsellors are about their work, and how much job satisfaction they derive. Even annual leave tends to be underused and must be consistently carried over to the next financial year.

The above recognition from practitioners on the ground has led to my accessing a public platform from which to promote Pretreatment and Pre-treatment Therapy. For example, under the auspices of the Great Chapel Street Medical Centre, where I am based, I was recently interviewed by the *British Medical Journal* (BMJ). Over the years I have spoken at numerous public events including the Royal College of Physicians of Ireland, the Royal College of Psychiatry, and the Faculty for Homeless and Inclusion Health. I believe that this has been possible because over the decades there has grown an awareness that homelessess, and the associated psychological factors both leading to and emanating from it have proved to be intractable. This opened minds up to the promise of novel approaches, such as Pretreatment and Pre-treatment Therapy.

To quote Kuhn (1962, p, 64):

> All crises [intractable problems or "anomalies"] begin with the blurring of a paradigm and the consequent loosening of the rules for normal research... [and] a crisis may end with the emergence of a new candidate for paradigm and with the ensuing battle over its acceptance.

Uncertainty arises when anomalies—discrepancies between the explanation given by the prevailing paradigm and the phenomenon it purports to explain—cast doubt on the established paradigm and leads to a period of "extraordinary science" where multiple paradigms compete until a consensus paradigm emerges (Hendersen & Tendler, 2017).

It might just be quite possible that Pretreatment is such a candidate in the field of homelessness, but that for it to meaningfully engage in the "battle for acceptance," it needs to develop its own bridging language, one based on research.

An evidence-based approach germane to Pretreatment is that of Attachment Theory (Bowlby 1975; 1982a; 1982b) and Modern Attachment Theory (Bateman & Fonagy, 2012; 2016; Schore, 2019), in that it is of the view that:

"...all ways of interacting in close relationships—also the ones that are inappropriate or difficult to participate in—have their origin in meaningful reactions to particular relational environments." (Daniel, 2015, p. 170). This includes traumatizing relationships.

Attachment Theory is now well established and has an impressive empirical research base, which has identified four specific styles of interacting and relating to people (attachment): Secure, Avoidant, Ambivalent, and Disorganised, the last three being insecure relational styles. The Disorganized style is the most challenging, and correlates with personality disorder or a "traumatised personality."

Daniel outlines interpersonal and narrative markers for each of the four relational styles, and since there is some evidence (Daniel, 2015, pp. 61-62) that insecure relational styles can develop into "learned secure attachment styles" (most commonly because of psychotherapy) these markers can be seen to evolve from one attachment style to another. Therefore, why not use a similar approach to Jay's Pretreatment stages?

Relational markers across the four attachment styles are: Tolerance of proximity/distance, Trust in others, Attitude to seeking and receiving help, expression and regulation (management) of emotions, Self-image/esteem, Openness and self-disclosure, Dependence/independence, Conflict management, and Empathy.

Narrative markers which vary across the four attachment styles are: Coherence and credibility, Balance in descriptions, Dramatization/minimization, Description of emotions, Abstraction/specificity, Consideration of listener, Verbosity, Narrative orderliness, Mentalization (self and others described as thinking and feeling).

Jay has already alluded to some possible markers for different Pretreatment stages (see chapter 1 and 3) and maybe some of the above could be included. The point is that a tool could be developed to follow the progress made through the stages—a tool open to quantification. For example, short five-point scales for each marker could be developed like for trust, or hope, aspiration or "learned helplessness" (Seligman, 2016), which occurs when someone has experienced repeated challenges and comes to believe they have no control over their situation. They then give up trying to make changes and accept their fate.[33] These brief scales can be scored either by the individual or the worker. Thus, meaningful quantitative indices of change can be designed and developed to present the impact of Pretreatment—the beginnings of a desperately needed bridging language between practitioners and commissioners.

Conclusion

Pretreatment and Pre-treatment Therapy truly meet people where they are at, suspending judgement, building trust, and taking their interpretation of their lives and their aspirations seriously and compassionately. With its open-ended time frame of support, this approach identifies the fissures in people's psychic homes. This enables the possibility for remedial healing, allowing for the possibility of not only rehousing but crucially, *sustainable homemaking*. Something we should all somehow have the right to do...

> "Warren" she said, "He has come home to die:
> You needn't be afraid he'll leave you this time."
>
> "Home," he mocked gently.
>
> "Yes, what else but home?
> It all depends on what you mean by home.
> Of course he's nothing to us, anymore
> Than was the hound that came a stranger to us
> Out of the woods, worn out upon the trail."
>
> "Home is the place where, when you have to go there,
> They have to take you in."
>
> "I should have called it
> Something you somehow haven't to deserve".
>
> Robert Frost, *The Death of the Hired Man* (1914)

[33] https://www.verywellmind.com/what-is-learned-helplessness-2795326, 09/03/24

References

The American Psychiatric Association's *Diagnostic and Statistical Manual of Mental Disorders* (DSM) - https://psycnet.apa.org/record/2013-14907-000, accessed 1st August 2023.

Bateman, A., Fonagy, P. (2012). *Handbook of mentalizing in mental health practice*. Washington, DC: American Psychiatric Publishing, Inc.

Bateman, A., Fonagy, P. (2016). *Mentalization-based treatment for borderline personality disorder: A practical guide*. Oxford, UK: Oxford University Press.

Bowlby, J. (1982a). *Attachment: Attachment and loss*. Basic Books Classics, Vol 1. New York, NY: Basic Books.

Bowlby, J. (1982b). *Loss: Sadness and depression*. Basic Books Classics, Vol 3. New York, NY: Basic Books.

Bowlby, J. (1975). *Separation: Anxiety and anger*. Basic Books Classics, Vol 2. New York, NY: Basic Books.

Cameron, R., (2020). *Working with difference & diversity in counselling and psychotherapy*. London, UK: Sage.

Cognitive Behaviour Therapy – CBT, (Accessed 2 September, 2023). https://www.nhs.uk/mental-health/talking-therapies-medicine-treatments/talking-therapies-and-counselling/cognitive-behavioural-therapy-cbt/overview/

Conolly, J.M.P. (2018a) "Pre-treatment Therapy: A Central London Counselling Services' Enhanced Response to Complex Needs Homelessness." Chapter 4, pp 49-66, in *Cross-cultural dialogues on homelessness: From pretreatment strategies to psychologically informed environments*. Edited by Jay S. Levy, with Robin Johnson. Ann Arbor, Michigan: LH Press.

Conolly, J.M.P., (2018b). "Pre-treatment Therapy Approach for Single Homeless People—The Co-construction of Recovery/Discovery," Chapter 6, pp 109-133 in *Social exclusion, compound trauma and recovery: Applying psychology, psychotherapy and PIE to homelessness and complex needs*. Ed, Peter Cockersell. London, UK: Jessica Kingsley Publishers.

Daniel, S., I., F. (2015). *Adult Attachment Patterns In A Treatment Context—Relationship and Narrative*. New York, NY: Routledge.

Hendersen, J., and Tendler, J. (2017). *An analysis of Thomas Kuhn's The structure of scientific revolutions*. New York, NY: Routledge.

Herman, J. (2015). *Trauma and recovery: The aftermath of violence from domestic abuse to political terror*. New York, NY: Basic Books

Holmes, J., (2006). *The search for the secure base—Attachment theory and psychotherapy. 5th edition*, London, UK: Routledge.

Holmes, J. & Slade, A. (2018). *Attachment in therapeutic practice*. London, UK: Sage.

HomeLink: Published, 22 May, 2021 https://www.homeless.org.uk/facts/homelessness-in-numbers/rough-sleeping/rough-sleeping-our-analysis.

Johns, D.F., Ricon, J.L.O. & Dommers, E. (2021). A continuum of harm: How systemic interactions can multiply and entrench complex disadvantage. Essay One, in *The knot: An essay collection on the interconnectedness of poverty, trauma, and multiple disadvantage*. London, UK: Revolving Doors Agency.

Kuhn, T. (1962). *The Structure of Scientific Revolutions*. 1970, 2nd Edition, University of Chicago, Illinois: Chicago Press.

Levy, J. S., (2010). *Homeless narratives & pretreatment pathways—From words to housing*. Ann Arbor, Michigan: LH Press.

Levy, J. S., (2013). *Pretreatment Guide for Homeless Outreach & Housing First*. Ann Arbor, Michigan: LH Press.

Levy, J. S. (2018). *Cross-cultural dialogues on homelessness: From pretreatment strategies to psychologically informed environments*. Eds, Jay S. Levy and Robin, Johnson. Ann Arbor, Michigan: LH Press.

Levy, J. S. (2021). *Pretreatment in action: Interactive exploration of homelessness to housing stabilization.* Ann Arbor, Michigan: LH Press.

Miller, W. R., and Rollnick, S., (2013), *Motivational Interviewing—Helping People Change.* New York, NY: The Guildford Press.

NHS Search, (Accessed 1 August, 2023). https://uk.search.yahoo.com/search?fr=mcafee&type=E211GB384G0&p=what+is+the+nhs

NICE Guideline CG78, (2009) *Borderline personality disorder: recognition and management.* (Accessed 15 July, 2023). https://www.nice.org.uk/guidance/cg78/chapter/2-Research-recommendations#psychological-therapy-programmes-for-people-with-borderline-personality-disorder

Net Doctor – UK Health Services, (Accessed 2 September, 2023). https://www.netdoctor.com.uk/health-services/nhs/a4489/what-is-the-nhs/

Prochaska, J. O. & Norcross, J. C., (2003). *'Systems of psychotherapy—A transtheoretical analysis,* 5th Ed. San Francisco, CA: Thompson-Brooks/Cole.

SAMHSA's Trauma and Justice Strategic Initiative (2014). *SAMHSA's Concept of Trauma and Guidance for a Trauma-Informed Approach.* https://store.samhsa.gov/sites/default/files/d7/priv/sma14-4884.pdf, accessed 09.05.2021

Schore, A. N. (2019). *The development of the unconscious mind.* New York, NY: W.W. Norton & Company.

Schore, A. N. (2019). *Right brain psychotherapy.* New York, London: W.W. Norton & Company

Seligman ME. Learned helplessness at fifty: Insights from neuroscience. *Psychology Rev.* 2016;123(4):349-367. doi:10.1037/rev0000033

Wagner, C. C., and Ingersoll, K. S., (2013). *Motivational interviewing in groups.* New York, NY: The Guildford Press.

9 A Workforce Development Programme: Working Effectively with People with Complex Trauma Histories Experiencing Multiple Disadvantages

Dr Ray Middleton

> I feel more at ease working with highly complex individuals. I think I have become more compassionate toward them and able to see the world through their lens better than before the training.
>
> Attendee of Ladder4Life training, 2024

I have had the privilege of working for over three decades in services attempting to reach out and be helpful to those people most marginalised in our society. They face multiple disadvantages, have often been without a home, experience unemployment, have longstanding struggles with their mental health connected to significant unresolved trauma, which is combined with problematic substance use, addictions of one kind or another, and other issues. I found it is extremely hard work to do well. There is significant emotional "wear and tear," both on those trying to reach out and be helpful and the people experiencing multiple difficulties and disadvantages.

Yet I remain both optimistic and enthusiastic about the work. During my youth, I was caught up in that retraumatising circle myself and it has helped maintain my motivation for decades. I had been written off as someone who could not get better, "poor prognosis" as my psychiatrist used to say. In my 20s, a psychiatrist told me I would not be employed again as my problems were "too deep-seated and complex." I led what many called a "chaotic life" in and out of scrapes—long term unemployed for years, socially isolated with no friends. I had problematic substance addictions, and had been an inpatient in the local psychiatric hospital seven times and received seven different mental health diagnoses and a wide range of prescribed psychiatric drugs from within the dominant biomedical model of mental health.

It did seem like I was caught up in a vicious cycle without a way out. I first came in contact with homeless services when I hitchhiked 3,000 miles across the trans-Canadian highway. The Salvation Army put me up on my journey. The roots of these difficulties lay both in my childhood trauma and my reactions to these traumas—the things I did in order to survive. Thankfully for me my psychiatrist was wrong, and I found ways to escape and navigate away from the *Negative Narrative* I was caught within. With help I found a way to build a more positive narrative to live my life within.

With a lot of help from other people, I found ways to get better and live the "good life" I had hoped to achieve. I got married and raised children and they had children, so now I am a proud Dad and Granddad. Whilst raising a family and working with people with multiple disadvantages, I also did a Ph.D., looking at trauma-informed and narrative/dialogical alternatives to the diagnosis of Personality Disorder. Once I escaped unemployment, I have not stopped working. Part of my motivation for the work is the experience of how painful it is to be stuck in a hopeless retraumatising cycle. How great it is to get out, get some help, make some changes and "get a life!" I think this is what we often hope for people, that they too can get a life and fulfil their potential in this world.

Another sustainer of my motivation and hope for this kind of work over the years has been my good fortune to come across a range of innovative, interesting and exciting person-centred, strengths-based approaches. These approaches, such as Pretreatment, Power Threat Meaning Framework, Psychologically Informed Environments, and Narrative psychology amongst others, help people facing multiple disadvantages in our society. Some of these ideas helped me see how consumer capitalist societies increase the negative social judgements of people who do not fit into the "individualistic thriving/successful" narratives promoted within our culture. We live in a highly unequal society, not just around socio-economic status with widening differences between the rich and the poor, but differences between the employed and the unemployed, the healthy and the ill, and so on. Increasingly, our society appears to promote narratives that stigmatise and encourage social evaluative negative judgements toward groups of people who don't fit society's "individual successful life" stories.

The explanations available in our culture when things go wrong in our lives are predominantly individualistic and self-blaming, such as: "I am a failure/What is wrong with me?" rather than "What has happened to me?" Society's narratives with negative social evaluative judgements of the "other" include judgement of; the "mentally ill," the "homeless," the "addict," the "immigrant," the "criminal," the "unemployed," and so on, and so on. These popularised narratives with negative judgements are accompanied by all kinds of powerful sets of ideas (ideology/ways of thinking) and practices from powerful institutions that make it harder for the individual to move from being in a repetitive cycle of emotional pain and pain-killing behaviours.

It is in this world I have had the privilege of working for over thirty years in a variety of roles, such as housing support, addictions counsellor, Care Coordinator in an Early Intervention in Psychosis service (in the UK), managing services and then managing managers of services, such as "Personality Disorder Accommodation" services. Doing these kinds of jobs got me curious about two questions:

1. Why was it often very difficult for me and my colleagues to work effectively with people with multiple disadvantages?
2. Why was it so difficult and rare for people with multiple difficulties and disadvantages to navigate their way from one world to another, from a pain-full world of repetitive re-traumatisation, of troubled and troubling behaviour into their preferred life—"the good life" they desired?

Over the years, I was fortunate to come across a number of innovative approaches and attempts to answer these questions from across Europe, Russia, the U.K. and the U.S.A. I have now combined my learning journey from these methodologies into a five-day workforce development programme I deliver to staff in services working with people with complex combinations of needs.

My hope is the combining of these novel methods will better equip helpers doing the important task of reaching out to people facing multiple disadvantages, whether that is friends, family, volunteers, peer support or paid staff in services. I have found that there is a great deal of emotional "wear and tear" doing this kind of work and often staff have their own unresolved trauma to process at the same time as trying to help others. In the last service I helped to manage, we had 10% of the people accessing our service die. This takes an emotional toll on the staff who are building relationships of trust with people often engaged in chaotic lives and health-harming habits that sometimes lead to death, or life-changing injuries. I have observed that these health-harming habits are often understandably formed in reaction to powerful threats and traumas as ways to survive the threats, but later turn into problematic habits and not helpful ones. Experiencing the emotional wear and tear on staff wellbeing prompted me to include self-care practices alongside the skills and knowledge that help them reach out more effectively.

What I have learnt so far is a drop, and the things I haven't learnt yet is an ocean, but I've put into this workforce development programme everything I know. The University of Lincoln undertook an independent research evaluation of the programme's effect on staff (Smith, Mason, and Dagnall, 2024). I am very pleased to report their findings reflect the very positive and enthusiastic feedback staff have given directly to me about the training as follows:

> Despite pre-existing high levels of knowledge and confidence amongst training participants, there was significant change in a number of areas, including significantly higher understanding of the term "trauma," and trauma-informed practice, and the impact of trauma on a person; significantly higher knowledge of the Power Threat Meaning Framework; significantly higher confidence in working with people who have experienced trauma; significantly higher perceived ability to work in a trauma-informed way; and significantly less likelihood of reporting feeling triggered when talking about trauma.
>
> —University of Lincoln College of Health and Science, Research Evaluation Report on The Ladder4Life Workforce Development Programme. February 2024

This training programme is based around a simple image (see Fig. 8-1) of going on a life-journey or Quest-narrative:

Fig 8-1: The Quest Narrative

Narrative Understanding and Competence

First, I teach staff about taking Narrative approaches to the work. I encourage people to reflect on themselves, and not just focus on understanding the people we hope to reach out to. We cannot help others effectively if we cannot have an honest reflection on ourselves and how we navigate our way through life through our own narratives. I find it hard to remember things I learn on training programmes, so I have created a visual image of someone going on a journey to get to the top of a mountain. This is basically a ***Quest Narrative*** structured around six simple questions on the image. I've reproduced the image here (see Fig. 8-1 on p. 169). Through a variety of reflective exercises, we explore together how personal narratives work. The key points are memorable through a mnemonic, which is "**A B C D E**"

"**A**" stands for *Ask good Questions*, such as

1. "What are your best hopes—the preferred future you want?" Or put another way, "How would you like your life to be better in your future?"
2. What and Who is in the Way? (of your preferred future)
3. What and Who Helps you on your Quest? (for this "good life" / "better life")
4. What emotions get stirred up when you go on, or even think about, this Quest? (Hope, frustration, annoyance, fear of failure, anxiety, shame, guilt, joy, low mood, etc.)
5. What is the Story so Far? and
6. What is my next Step?

"**A**" also stands for helpful Additional follow up Questions. In any of these six areas, we can ask further questions, such as: "Is there Anything Else?" ('that might help ...that might get in the way ...anything else about this "Good Life" you hope for). Such follow up questions can enrich and embed each part of a more hopeful **Quest-narrative**. This draws on ideas from narrative psychology and Solution Focused Practice.

"**B**" stands for Bigger and Smaller Stories. We can lend our capacity to be curious to someone else in conversation. Once we start to get a rough idea of one Quest someone would like to go on to get a better life (The "Good Life!") then we can think together with them about whether this Quest is connected to any bigger or smaller stories in their life. For example, someone may have an initial qualification/educational type Quest to pass their driving test or get a Catering Qualification. This may connect to a bigger Employment-type Quest narrative (to get a paid job driving or be a chef). They may combine these quests, as someone I was working with did into a desire to "run their own burger van one day." The initial Quest someone sketches out may have smaller subplots or mini quests that need to be completed in order to reach their valued Bigger Goal, such as addressing a substance use issue in order to reach their desired Goal, which could be fulfilling a family role, like "Being a Good Dad/Mom."

Next in this mnemonic, "**C**" stands for Complementary Stories. These are any Positive Stories that support and resonate well with the original Quest. Wanting to fulfil a family role may be an example of this, so this core/key Value is good to tune into if the person we are working with voices that this is important to them. This can help to build motivation, to help connect and link personal narratives and values together. We may say, "So I hear you saying your Quest to get a paid job as a chef is important to you because it is going to help you be a better Dad or Mom to your children. Have I understood you right?"

However, when I am teaching about personal narratives, the "**C**" also stands for the opposite: Conflicting Narratives. Often people are very conflicted, and we can all be. Part of them believes they could work toward their preferred "best-hopes" future ("I could get a home, a decent job, a relationship, be a good Mum/Dad, etc.") with support, but part of them also believes some conflicting negative narratives about themselves. Examples are, "I'm a loser, smack head, I'll never amount to anything," or "I'll never get a job because I'm a schizophrenic!" Often powerful negative narratives have been produced outside the person in their wider social world, either by other people in emotionally abusive ways, or by powerful institutions they have had contact with.

Either way, it is often useful to explore the Conflicting Narratives people believe. With help we can pivot away from, and disbelieve, any negative personal narrative we are entrapped within, but only if we have a more positive narrative to replace them with—we need a better story to pivot into. Stories only have power over us whilst we believe them. When we stop believing them, they lose their power over us. But we do need an alternative narrative to jump into instead—we won't jump into a vacuum of space/time.

The "**D**" prompts us to examine the value of considering our personal narratives because "narratives Define us:" they shape our thoughts, feelings and behaviours. But it is also worth considering "the Danger of a single story," since some stories unfairly entrap and prevent people reaching their full potential, including narratives in our culture about members of groups society evaluates and judges negatively, such as those without a home, a job, those with a "mental disorder," addiction issues, or ex-offenders. We may take up habitation in a narrative created by other people or institutions.

The "**E**" reminds us that we sometimes have confusing Experiences involving our thoughts, feelings and behaviours that we then try to fit into a narrative explanation. We tap into our culture to find a narrative explanation, and some narratives are more dominant and easier to find than others. Some narratives are given more authority in our culture and so are more likely to author our experiences, but becoming aware we are authored opens up possibilities of changing our personal narrative. We also explore ways we can co-Edit and co-create new narratives with other people as we open up a dialogue about how they see themselves and their situation. We all co-Edit and co-create our personal narratives all the time during conversations about the ups and downs of our life with others. This is a normal process. We apply some principles from Open Dialogue developed in Western Lapland such as accepting we only ever partly know what is going on. We also explore some other concepts from the Russian theorist Mikhail Bakhtin and his Dialogical approach.

The Power Threat Meaning Framework

After establishing a good understanding of Narrative approaches, we layer on top of this an exploration of the Power Threat Meaning Framework (Boyle & Johnstone, 2020). This is a person-centred, holistic alternative to the dominant Bio-medical diagnostic approach to mental distress. It helps staff consider how power might be operating in their lives and the lives of the people they are reaching out to serve. We explore what access to powerful resources people have and what powerful threats there may be to people getting their needs met. A wide range of different types of power is explored, and how they may interact, including; Economic, Material, Legal, Interpersonal, Social/Group, Biological, and Ideological Power. This allows consideration of how capitalism works in our society.

Habits of behaviour, thinking and emotions that may be interpreted as "symptoms of a disorder" within the Bio-medical model, are instead reconceptualised through the PTMF as understandable "Threat Responses." These are understandable responses to the powerful threats people face and have faced in their past; habits formed through what people have had to do in order to survive threatening situations. The focus is on exploring the meaning people are making of their experiences and situations.

Trauma-Informed approaches

Next, we explore Trauma-Informed approaches and consider how trauma-reactions can affect a wide range of areas for both staff and the people they serve. Some of these areas are our Thinking, Emotions, Body (Somatization), Behaviour, and patterns of Relating with others. Everything covered is related back to the Quest Image and how these skills and knowledge may help someone on their life journey. We explore a number of approaches including those promoted by Substance Abuse and Mental Health Services Administration (SAMHSA, 2014). Matt Bennett in chapter 2 of this book provides an extensive overview of Trauma-Informed Care.

Pretreatment

From this firm foundation, we dive into the excellent set of skills outlined in Jay Levy's Pretreatment approach (Levy, 2021). Each of the principles of Pretreatment proves to be a rich springboard to open up dialogue. An example is how common language construction provokes excellent reflection and discussion. We need to cross a cultural divide from our own house of language to the other's house of language, and then perhaps bridge into the language and jargon of services. We then link this to the philosopher Miranda Fricker's concept of Epistemic

Injustice... people facing multiple disadvantages belong to many groups, and may be given less credibility due to this. We explore the experience of sexual exploitation of young women and girls by gangs of men in the UK to build cultural competence and skills around cross-cultural communication. This also highlights how legal and ideological power can work. We also consider different approaches to risk using the Pretreatment principle of increasing safety. Then we examine therapeutic risk taking and how organisations tend to be risk-averse, often unintentionally restricting the work they are aiming to achieve. Pretreatment also provides excellent principles that promote reflective practice through Supportive Supervision or Co-vision leading to rich discussion and in-depth exploration. Jay Levy provides a detailed review of Pretreatment and its five principles of care in chapters 1 and 3.

Psychologically Informed Environments

We also cover the principle of PIE, Psychologically Informed Environments, using these points to empower and motivate staff to improve the service they work for. There are natural links among many of the topics covered. For example, the "Spaces of Opportunity" lead naturally into reflection and discussion around the wider system, system change and systemic thinking. We also think about getting the most out of Group Reflective Practice and consider different models of reflective practice. Robin Johnson reviews PIE and its relationship with Pretreatment in chapter 5.

Addiction and How to Manage our own Anxiety and stay emotionally centred

A very fruitful day of the programme is spent looking at different approaches to a variety of types of addiction, and how to stay emotionally centred doing this challenging work, with an in-depth look at how to Manage our own Anxiety—and techniques to help others to better manage their Anxiety.

Conclusion

The United Nation's and World Health Organisation's joint report into mental health and human rights (2023) concluded that part of the current difficulties in helping people in mental distress is the over-reliance on the Bio-medical model of distress, focusing on diagnosis and medication. They called for an urgent move away from the current over-reliance on the Bio-medical model to more person centred, holistic, rights-based approaches. This programme is in keeping with this aim as the P.T.M.F. is explicitly an alternative to the diagnostic approach. We look at the research evidence supporting such a shift by considering the work of Robert Whitaker[34] (www.madinamerica.com). This leads to the research of the British psychiatrist, Joanna Moncrieff, on the myth of the chemical imbalance theory to help understand how ideological power works through forces such as Big Pharmaceutical companies. We also cautiously look at trans-generational trauma, both through socialisation and through Epigenetics, exploring the new and emerging evidence that the social traumas our grandparents went through may have altered the expression (switched tags) of our DNA.

The development of the programme has involved many collaborative experiences. I am very grateful that my learning journey so far includes the opportunity to meet and work with likeminded innovators and disrupters like Jay Levy (Pretreatment), Robin Johnson (PIE) and Lucy Johnstone (PTMF) and many others, including people who identify as "experts by experience," whose ideas have helped shape my ongoing thinking and practice in the work.

If you have any comments or questions or would like to know more about my workforce development programme, just email me at: Ray.middleton@ladder4life.com

References

Boyle, M. & Johnstone, L. (2020). *A straight-talking introduction to the Power Threat Meaning Framework*. PCCS Books: Wales, UK.

Levy, J. S. (2021). *Pretreatment in action: Interactive exploration of homelessness to housing stabilization*. Ann Arbor, MI: Loving Healing Press.

[34] *Mad in America* was originally started by the scientific journalist Robert Whitaker. An excellent interview with him discussing his investigation of how the Bio-medical model has grown to dominate Western capitalist countries, the links between Big Pharmaceutical companies and the creation of diagnosis can be seen here: https://youtu.be/F5n2SM8SH88

Smith, L., Mason, R. & Dagnall, R. (2024) *Ladder4Life Training Evaluation*. External Report. University of Lincoln: England, UK. https://repository.lincoln.ac.uk/articles/report/Ladder4Life_Report_Feb_2024/25249381

Referenced Websites

Mad in America: Good resources looking critically at the scientific research behind the Bio-medical model can be found at www.madinamerica.com

Mental Health, Human Rights and Legislation: Guidance and Practice, (2023) United Nation's and World Health Organisation's (WHO) report into mental health. The launch film here: https://www.youtube.com/live/eLzErwWyvLw

Dr Ray Middleton*:* Lots of video resources on my YouTube Channel, such as my presentation to a government conference on reaching people with multiple disadvantages, here: https://www.youtube.com/watch?v=yQT4VRL5IOc

Joanna Moncrieff (British psychiatrist) has a website: https://joannamoncrieff.com

Here is an excellent interview with Joanna where she discusses "The Myth of The Chemical Imbalance" and its origins serving Big Pharma companies, link here: https://www.youtube.com/watch?v=FdbX5JstwgA

The Power Threat Meaning Framework Resources can be found online at: https://www.bps.org.uk/member-networks/division-clinical-psychology/power-threat-meaning-framework

Pretreatment: Lots of useful information and links to Jay Levy's books on his website, https://www.jayslevy.com

Psychologically Informed Environments (PIE): Lots of free resources and a free sign up at: https://pielink.net

Substance Abuse and Mental Health Services Administration (SAMHSA) strategic Initiative, (2014) SAMHSA's Concept of trauma and guidance for a trauma informed approach. https://ncsacw.acf.hhs.gov/userfiles/files/SAMHSA_Trauma.pdf

10 The Universality of Pretreatment

Jay S. Levy

> Diversity is about personalised shades of experience emanating from universal colours of humanity, but each person takes from the universal what is relevant to them and alters it by their own interpersonal experience.
>
> Camila Batmanghelidjh (2010)

A Pretreatment framework values collaborative and inclusive relationships on all levels. We promote productive dialogue by building a Person-Centered relationship that is respectful of a person's culture, ideals, and experience. It's a challenge that we can take on with a sense of awe and wonder for what we may discover and what could come to be. Whether it is crossing cultural divides to work effectively with other systems of care, or establishing pathways to services and resources within our own system of care, or in our direct service to those in need, or supporting our staff through reflective practice, building person-centered relationships is at the foundation of what we do. As demonstrated in previous chapters, through the application of the five universal principles and processes of care, Pretreatment guides and can transform our work.

The five Pretreatment principles of care discussed previously are:

1. Relationship formation via the Stages of Engagement
2. Common Language Construction: Stages are Understanding, Utilizing and Bridging

3. Ecological Considerations: Transition and Adaptation process to ideas, people, and environments
4. Promoting Safety through Crisis Intervention and Harm Reduction Strategies
5. Facilitating Change through Change Model and Motivational Interviewing Strategies

Pretreatment is attentive to people's narratives, joining with a person's sense of meaning rather than working against it. The effectiveness of this approach transcends the world of homelessness and is applicable across multiple fields of practice. Pretreatment resonates broadly throughout our diverse human service networks regardless of mission, setting, or the people we are called to serve. This is because the common element to the success or failure of most, if not all human service endeavors is the strength and health of our relationships.

Universal Themes and Individualization

Here, we have brought together a variety of authors from the US and UK to explore the many applications of Pretreatment. By doing so, we reviewed other approaches of universal value throughout these pages. Whether it be Matt Bennett's discussion of Trauma-Informed Care (TIC), or Robin Johnson's development of the Psychologically Informed Environments movement and its many applications, or Dr Ray Middleton's well-designed staff training program from the perspectives of both "expert from experience" and expert in the field, they have all benefited by integrating a Pretreatment approach. Each has become ever more whole by working in harmony with Pretreatment. This universal flexible quality of Pretreatment means it can be added to and integrated with other psychological models to achieve this greater whole.

A Pretreatment approach is particularly helpful when working with highly vulnerable populations who are often pre-contemplative of treatment or recovery-based options of care. This is where Pretreatment shines, and the chapters by Virginia Bilz on Special Education in the public schools, and Kate Shapiro on case management and the challenges of tenancy preservation, and Daniel Southhall's and Chris Brown's writing on Pre-treatment Therapy really speak to this. Notably, this is done in tandem with highlighting how Pretreatment revitalized their work by adding a newfound sense of direction and meaning.

As a supervisor, I have found through reflective practice that staff really value a Pretreatment approach, because it upholds their creativity and purpose. Its principles are both universal and flexible enough to promote general guidance and individualization. It is therefore not overly prescriptive as to exactly how staff should intervene. Instead, it provides a tool for greater enquiry and exploration with a deeper understanding and insight that generates new ideas that may arise from a particular specialty or expertise that participants and staff bring to the table. It provides more fertile grounding for improving the methods and processes to achieve our mission. It gives staff the tools to clearly identify progress and success. It can boost their professional self-worth, resulting in the endurance to continue doing the work with clear eyes, grace, and hope.

We often miss opportunities for positive change when stuck in our pre-formed clinical assessments based on people's deficits or limited by the scope of our professional language. The special sauce of Pretreatment is the way it helps staff, participants or clients, and even program managers and administrators, across the spectrum of human services to get "unstuck." This is accomplished through the understanding and communication inherent to person-centered relationships. We thereby see a fuller picture based on people's narratives and are empowered to step into the great unknown of open dialogue to support our efforts to co-produce creative solutions.

Conclusion

As we look toward the future, the universal applications of a Pretreatment model can and has led to some exciting hybrids to help inform clinical care, advocacy, and staff training. John Conolly's chapter summarizes the evolution of one such hybrid, Pre-treatment Therapy. John suggests the need for a paradigm shift by implementing a Pretreatment philosophy and practice, rather than being wedded to the traditional medical model, when serving people who are entrenched in homelessness and have experienced significant trauma. He discusses the ramifications of people not having access to care and/or the Toxic Help inflicted by well-meaning mental health clinicians who follow standard clinical practice. People are often screened out due to not meeting a specified readiness criterion, or, if accepted, staff may cause unintended harm by facilitating another failed helping relationship. Pretreatment Therapy poses a way forward that is more inclusive for this often ill-served or virtually ignored population. Across the spectrum of services Pretreatment can open the door to greater access.

In *Cross-Cultural Dialogues on Homelessness* (2018, p. 66) John Conolly states,

> Pretreatment and Pre-treatment therapy are terribly exciting developments in that they offer a key to enabling a greater range of excluded groups in through the door. It wouldn't at all surprise me for further Pretreatment derivatives to emerge, such as Pre-treatment Schema Therapy (for PD), or Pre-treatment CBT (for anxiety and depression), or Pre-treatment Interpersonal Therapy (for depression), or Pre-treatment Eye Movement Desensitisation Therapy (EMDR for PTSD). The list goes on and on...

Beyond what has been discussed in these chapters, Pretreatment has also been utilized to better serve folks with complex and multiple needs in a variety of programs such as After Incarceration Services, Street Medicine,[35] Housing First Programs, and Peer Recovery settings, etc. In closing, Pretreatment is a transformative approach that can open the door to serve so many of those who need/want assistance, yet are reticent to receive help, or even if they find the words or strike up the courage to ask, they don't receive the quality of care they deserve.

As Robin Johnson states in a previous chapter,

> Jay's work helped to pinpoint what I came to call the core skills in engagement, those that are needed in any setting, whether in one to one work, in street outreach, or in any advice centre, day centre, shelter, or in ongoing support to individuals in their own

---

[35] In my previous book, *Pretreatment In Action: Interactive Exploration of Homelessness to Housing Stabilization* (2021), Joel Hunt wrote the foreword and shared the impact of Pretreatment on his Street Medicine practice in Fort Worth, Texas. In this book, Dr Jim Withers, the founder of the Street Medicine Institute, penned the US foreword.

homes. In all the steps on the pathway to settled accommodation, I suggest, these skills will be in play. In fact, even in explicitly therapeutic work, in actual "treatment," I would argue that these skills are essential. Without that original engagement, no other techniques can get traction.

I am thankful to all those who have contributed to this book, and to those who have taken the time to apply this model to their practice. I hope that the reader considers relevant applications of Pretreatment, whatever their field of practice, as well as how they engage with people in their daily lives by upholding and reaching for the promise of productive dialogue and healing relationships.

References

Batmanghelidjh, C. (2010). Child Centred Practice: Looking for the sandwich in the therapy room. Chapter 4, pp. 33-42 in *Anti-discriminatory practice in counselling and psychotherapy*. Lago, C., & Smith, B. Sage Publications Inc: Thousand Oaks, CA.

Levy, J. S. (2021). *Pretreatment in action: Interactive exploration of homelessness to housing stabilization*. Ann Arbor, MI: Loving Healing Press.

Levy, J.S. & Johnson, R. (2018). *Cross-cultural dialogues on homelessness: From pretreatment strategies to psychological environments*. Ann Arbor, MI: Loving Healing Press.

Appendix

Reflections and Testimonials

A Pretreatment approach is well aligned with my field experience and values. Through my twenty-seven years of work in various capacities under the human services umbrella, the importance of positive relationships rooted in mutual respect, trust, and shared goals cannot be overstated. The lessons I have learned throughout my career with respect to effectively engaging and supporting pre-contemplative individuals and families are easily translatable to executive level leadership.

It all starts with a connection—that spark that ignites the light in the darkness and creates hope. A person's story is so much more important to me than their pathology narrative. I am far less interested in someone's diagnosis, eviction history, behavioral health and medical history than learning about their life story, strengths, and dreams. I am particularly dialed into how the person has experienced services throughout life—what helped and what was difficult? When I have taught Clinical Practice at the graduate level and reviewed the stages of treatment: engagement, assessment, treatment, evaluation and termination; I made sure that students understood the importance of remaining in the engagement phase for several months if not years if needed. We must show we are genuinely interested in their identified needs and support preferences and collaboratively develop and operationalize a plan to move forward that makes sense to all involved.

When I first began working with Jay in 2018 at Eliot Community Human Services, I knew he was a kindred spirit within the first five minutes of our time together. His book, *Pretreatment Across Multiple Fields of Practice: Trauma Informed Approach to Homelessness and Beyond* (edited by Jay S. Levy, MSW with Louise Levy, MEd), was incredibly validating for me as it completely encapsulates my approach. While Jay's body of written work is truly inspiring, I count myself fortunate to be among the select few who got to watch his wisdom come to life in the form of supportive staff forums and client-facing work. Jay is a clinician's clinician and a gifted leader who has inspired countless field staff and leadership to see the best in people, even when there are understandable reasons not to. Jay's legacy as a leader, mentor, advocate, and practitioner has transformed thousands of lives for the better and I could not be happier to see his light continue to shine in the form of this wonderful collection of work.

Keith Wales, MSW, LICSW
Vice President of Homeless Services
Eliot Community Human Services

Insightful read, not only for my role supporting the population who are homeless in Westminster, but for me personally as someone who considers themselves a peer to this population.

This book has allowed me to gain a greater and more useful understanding of the need and value of Pretreatment for many of the clients we work with, alongside trauma-informed care.

The chapter on Neurobiology was of particular interest to me and how trauma disrupts the nervous system and brain development. Many of the clients I have worked with over the years have experienced past trauma, particularly in their developing years. The Cup and water analogy is a very visual and simple one for someone like myself who is not trained in mental health or psychology, but works with people who have or are currently experiencing trauma.

I would encourage anyone, whether you are supporting someone who has experienced trauma or maybe wishes to understand themselves, like I do, to read this book.

David Woodley
Westminster Homeless Health Care Navigator

It is my pleasure to recommend Jay Levy's new book, *Pretreatment Across Multiple Fields of Practice*. Having been a supervisor, program manager, and senior leader for over forty years in acute care settings in Western Massachusetts, I am deeply aware of the importance of stable, secure and safe housing in a person's journey to creating a rewarding and stable corner in this world.

I was often challenged by the question—how can we help folks get there? At times it is not even the absence of resources (which of course is real), but the lack of a trusted guide to outline a path. I had the good fortune of working with Jay and his staff in my last position as the Department of Mental Health Director for Hampshire County in Western Mass. There, Jay introduced me to his ideas around "Pretreatment." I intuitively resonated with the respect, dedication, and clinical soundness upon which these ideas are built. I quickly learned his staff were folks out there living out those ideals. They were walking the streets, fields, and meadows. Many times, if my clinical staff lost track of someone, Jay's staff could help with a recent sighting! Often, we worked together to bring a person into a relationship with us—the housing outreach clinician, and the "mental health system." It benefited our shared folks by meeting the person where they were with respect, relationship, and connection.

It is not a coincidence that mental health practitioners now understand trauma as often causing a life-changing rupture in human connection. Those "sleeping rough" (a term I learned from Jay) have had that rupture in the most primal sense from their "original tribe"... their family. It is not uncommon for those "sleeping rough," in unhoused settings, to form attachments to their fellow travelers who understand, withhold judgment, and form deep bonds based on facing issues of survival. The model of Pretreatment in my experience reaches across the divide of "otherness" that wounds and separates, and offers a hand to understand and invite a person into our community circle.

There is quite a bit of wisdom within these pages.

Anne Marie Martineau, MSSW, ACSW, LICSW

If I had a magic wand loaded with one wish, it would be for every human to become like the collection of authors of this book. Earth is in its sixth extinction event because of a global culture that rewards and encourages the worst in human nature, particularly greed and divisiveness. If this global culture magically changed into one that encourages the best in human nature, we would have a chance of survival, and a society in which homelessness and other woes would not exist.

A Shintoist saying is, "There are many mountains to God, and many paths up each mountain." This book has chapters describing a variety of approaches that are all based on respect, compassion, decency, patience, and acceptance. Individually, each is powerful. Combined, as this book recommends, they have the potential to transform the world.

Pretreatment Across Multiple Fields of Practice is necessary reading for anyone in any helping profession, in which I even include law enforcement, and highly recommended for everyone who wants a better world.

Bob Rich, PhD
Healesville, Victoria, Australia
Author of *From Depression to Contentment*

With their book *Pretreatment Across Multiple Fields of Practice:* Jay and Louise Levy and their remarkable team of co-authors have succeeded in distilling years of diverse experience serving people with complex psychological and physical needs into a much-needed roadmap for providers. Recognizing that human minds need models to tackle complex work, the manuscript clearly outlines working principles that guide practitioners in the art of building authentic and effective working partnerships with people experiencing homelessness and other traumas, while minimizing re-traumatization and creating psychological safety. Carefully chosen case studies beautifully illustrate how these principles can be put into practice in a variety of settings—from street outreach to shelters to special education classrooms—and are attentive to the impact of racism and other forms of oppression. The stories shared by the authors are powerful examples of the importance of building therapeutic alliances that are based on the radical notion that the people we are trying to help are the experts in their own lives.

Like many of the book's contributors, I wish I had learned of the Pretreatment model earlier in my career as its approach is transformative. This book should be required reading for everyone working in the human services field!

Kiko Malin, MPH, MSW
Public Health Director, Town of Amherst

As a staff member in the NHS, working in a service providing mental health provision for those who are rough sleeping and those at most risk of rough sleeping, Jay S. Levy's *Pretreatment Across Multiple Fields of Practice: Trauma Informed Approach to Homelessness and Beyond* is the book I have been waiting for.

Listening to the voices of actual professionals directly working with those experiencing complex trauma and multiple disadvantages, including NHS staff here in the UK, and hearing the challenges they face in a frank, open and honest way is extremely grounding, thought provoking and relatable.

I found it clever how Levy used Pretreatment values of collaboration and inclusive relationships throughout the book, utilising people's relevant experiences and strengths to promote wellbeing. Each contributing author shows their passion for the work, giving specific examples and providing the reader with feelings of validation, not shying away from honesty and transparency around their views, particularly around the NHS 'medical model.' So many times, I said "yes!" out loud in agreement whilst reading. Levy and company offer alternatives that work in, what they have found to be, effective ways throughout the chapters, described through the use of emotive case studies, offering more relational approaches which are very grounding and validating to hear. Weaving Pretreatment with Psychological Informed Environments and Trauma Informed Care movements presents the opportunity for us to revolutionise the ways we work with and support homeless communities.

This book emphasises that despite all the challenges faced, people working in this sector, me included, feel a genuine privilege to be working in this area and for the NHS, continuing to remain passionate and enthusiastic about the work we do. This book has validated my enthusiasm, my frustrations, my thoughts, and my approach to the work, to name a few. Jay S. Levy and co-authors have created a must read for everyone who works with those who are homeless and beyond.

Emma Marsh
Clinical Team Manager, LYPFT Rough Sleepers Mental Health Service
Chair of the nationwide Setting up Services Forum for Homelessness

This is key reading for any staff involved in providing care for people experiencing homelessness, especially those sleeping rough, and present with multiple and complex health and care issues. This book is relevant to workers from a range of disciplines such as health, housing, substance misuse, and care workers as well as commissioners. It follows on from the previous book, *Pretreatment In Action*, and this is reflected in the range of contributing authors. The different aspects of their contributions show a different way to work with individuals who present with multiple and complex issues.

Pretreatment Across Multiple Fields of Practice demonstrates that the traditional medical model does not meet the needs of individuals who present as being homeless. They are all too often seen as being too hard to engage with and it very clearly presents a better way of working that focuses on person centred and holistic care. The authors of this book strongly advocate for moving away from medical and siloed models of care where an individual is expected to fit into a medicalized system with a focus on key performance indicators, tick boxes and repeated assessments, which only retraumatise individuals leaving further damage and disengagement.

A Pretreatment approach focuses on principles that are person centred, holistic, and with a model that is strength-and-asset based with systems being solution focused and integrated. Through this psychosocial model of engagement, there is also a move away from discrimination, stigma, and blame to a model that is integrated and inclusive. There is opportunity for innovation with models and systems being co-designed and co-produced with service users. There is a move away from judgement to one of listening and acceptance.

Throughout, the book clearly shows how systems need to change to meet individuals' needs through a multi-disciplinary and integrated approach with principles of compassion, empathy, kindness, responsiveness, accessibility, flexibility, equity, as well as timeliness and accountability at the heart of delivery. To ensure that services are accessible, they need to be delivered through an outreach model. This will benefit individuals experiencing homelessness, as well as providers and commissioners on a personal level, while also delivering tremendous cost savings for providers and commissioners. The pre-treatment time is crucial for engagement, both immediately and in the longer term. Health is seen in the broadest sense with the social determinants of health and intersectionality being key components in addressing and delivering both immediate and longer-term care with a clear vision of hope and what can be achieved. This model not only has an impact on individuals experiencing homelessness, but also has an impact on workers preventing burn out with a greater sense of purpose, as well as the improvement in staff satisfaction and wellbeing.

Finally, this model can also benefit other inclusion health groups and can be used in areas where there is deprivation. The learning from this book and the Pretreatment model of engagement is a move towards healing and hope where trusted relationships can be built. Change is possible!

Jane Cook
Queen's Nurse, Registered General Nurse, Health Visitor
Complex Needs Manager, Groundswell

About the Authors

Jay S. Levy, MSW, LICSW
Clinical Social Worker, Consultant, Writer

Jay S. Levy has spent more than thirty years working with individuals who experience homelessness. He is the author of the highly acclaimed book *Pretreatment Guide for Homeless Outreach & Housing First* (2013). Jay's 2018 project was a collaborative effort with several authors from the UK entitled Cross-*Cultural Dialogues on Homelessness: From Pretreatment Strategies to Psychologically Informed Environments.* During 2021, Jay Published a workbook entitled *Pretreatment In Action: Interactive Exploration from Homelessness to Housing Stabilization.* He has also published *Homeless Narratives & Pretreatment Pathways* (2010), as well as a monograph (2011) and several journal articles on Homelessness issues.

Jay developed Pretreatment as an approach for helping people without homes who are often deemed "not ready" and excluded from housing and/or recovery-oriented services and treatment. While working with Eliot CHS Homeless Services, Jay has helped to create new Housing First programs such as the Regional Engagement and Assessment for Chronically Homeless program (REACH).

Jay has achieved formal recognition from the Commonwealth of Massachusetts Department of Mental Health for his past efforts to help under-served homeless individuals through his direct service, clinical supervision of staff, and program development. Jay received his MSW degree in clinical social work from Columbia University in 1988.

Jay lives in Western MA with his wife, Louise, who recently celebrated retirement after more than thirty years of teaching high school science, and was kind enough to provide valuable assistance in editing this book. Jay is very proud and excited for his daughters, Talia and

Sara, who have both graduated college and have embraced journeys into career-related activities and beyond.

More information on Jay's consultative work, presentations, and publications can be found at www.jayslevy.com

Louise Levy, MEd – Science Teacher

Louise, recently retired, was an outdoor Educator and High School Science teacher for over 40 years. Louise taught Biology, Chemistry, Physics, Astronomy, Anatomy, a variety of elective courses, and served as faculty Advisor for Ecomentors and the Environmental Club. She has had the distinct pleasure of helping thousands of students refine their delivery (and check their grammar and spelling) as they communicated through research-based papers and public service message-themed projects. Integrating meaningful exploration of local surroundings into the classroom has been her passion, helping students build a sense of place, self-determination, and community involvement. She is a veteran (16 years) of the Harvard Forest Schoolyard Ecology program, now serving as teacher-mentor. Recipient of multiple awards for excellence in teaching (Mass Audubon, Mass Agriculture in the Classroom, Mass Educators Hall of Fame) Louise has presented at numerous professional conferences and was director/grant writer for many grants supporting STEAM (Science, Technology, Engineering, Art, and Math) activities inside and outside of the classroom. Louise has happily served as a sounding board and participated in the editing process of Jay's various writing projects.

John Conolly, UKCP reg Psychoanalytic Psychotherapist, Lacanian Analyst, *MA (Psychoanalysis), MA (Psychology)*

John is a United Kingdom Council for Psychotherapy (UKCP) registered Psychoanalytic Psychotherapist, and Lacanian Analyst, and has taught on "the Psychology of Trauma and Therapeutic Skills" at the Tavistock and Portman NHS Trust, as well as at the Middlesex University, Mental Health Department.

He has helped manage a counselling charity for homeless people, worked as a (French) bi-lingual counsellor at a London NHS mental health trust "forced migration trauma service" (for asylum seekers and refugees), and for the last fifteen years has led the Central London

Community Healthcare NHS Trust "homeless health counselling service" in Westminster.

Together with an ex-service user, he introduced "walk in" counselling clinics, as well as anger support and discussion groups for rough sleepers. They also co-founded the "Westminster Complex Personalities Network," which, together with Robin Johnson and the Westminster "Rough Sleepers" commissioning team, was instrumental in introducing the PIE approach across Westminster homeless services.

John also introduced Pretreatment in his service and its application as "Pre-treatment Therapy," which he has spoken extensively about at conferences, and has authored several chapters and journal articles on. Several NHS psychological services have recently been commissioned to deliver Pretreatment across the country.

Being a passionate believer in empowering frontline workers with the appropriate mindset and skills to avoid retraumatising service users, he developed a trauma-informed skills training package, part of which was delivered on NHS England's national online platform. This was under the auspices of the national homeless and inclusion health charity, "Pathway." John consults to the "National forum for homeless mental health services," which Dan Southall founded in 2021. One present initiative is the development of meaningful, credible, and operational measures of psycho-social change in a homeless person's pretreatment journey of "recovery."

He is a committee member for the London mental health and homelessness steering group, as well as the University of Dublin, Trinity College Global Health Centre research project on "translational simulation for trauma informed care." Otherwise, John enjoys the diverse restaurants and jazz venues of north London, his family, and walking his little dog, Marley, around the many parks on offer.

Matthew Bennett, MBA, MA
Author, Trainer, Director of Optimal HRV

Matt Bennett is a renowned speaker, author, podcaster, and founder of Optimal HRV. He has over twenty-five years of experience and advanced mental health and leadership degrees. Matt's mission is to guide individuals and organizations in delivering exceptional healing-based solutions. He's an accomplished speaker and trainer, sharing his expertise at conferences, universities, and organizations nationwide. Matt's approach to integrating organizational management with trauma-informed care is groundbreaking, promoting resiliency and positive change among staff. His passion for fostering growth and healing is apparent in everything he does. You can contact him via matt@optimalhrv.com

Robin Johnson
Writer and Independent Researcher, Author of the PIE's Framework, Founder of PIElink.net

Robin Johnson is the principal author of the PIEs approach, having first coined the term when working as a policy analyst and development consultant with the UK Department of Health, Department of Communities and Local Government and the Cabinet Office.

Reflecting on the innovative approaches and practices he had observed in frontline homelessness services in the UK, Robin developed the PIEs ideas further, and later the PIEs practice framework to describe and facilitate these developments. This framework has since evolved, through continuous discussion and development with a growing community of practice and other stakeholders across the homelessness sector and the wider services environment in the UK and beyond.

Along with many other essays on PIEs, in 2023 Robin authored *Psychologically Informed Environments from the ground up: service design for complex needs*, the first comprehensive guide to developing services as PIEs, and to the PIElink (www.pielink.net), the PIE's on-line community of practice and resources hub.

Dr Ray Middleton, PhD
Staff Trainer and Founder of Ladder4Life

Dr Middleton has worked for over thirty years with the most socially excluded groups who have experienced multiple disadvantages combining trauma, mental health, substance misuse and housing needs. Ray is a member of the British Psychological Society (BPS) P.T.M.F. Steering Committee—and chairs their sub-committee on training. His PhD was on dialogical/narrative approaches to complex trauma, critiquing the history of the diagnosis of "Personality Disorder."

Previously, Ray has set up and managed "personality disorder" services, been a senior care coordinator in an early intervention in psychosis service, and is a systemic practitioner within systemic family therapy. Ray also has past personal lived experience of surviving complex childhood trauma, recovery from addiction, and using services within the psychiatric system—an experience that motivates him to write and deliver innovative training to improve staff skills and services for the most socially excluded groups.

Contact: Ray.middleton@ladder4life.com

Dr Dan Southall, DClinPsy, Msc, Bsc, CPsychol

Dan Southall has worked as a clinical psychologist in the NHS since qualifying in 2017. He is currently lead psychologist in the complex emotional service in North Lincolnshire. In his previous role in the Humber Homeless Mental Health Team, he worked alongside other professionals to develop one of the first psychologically informed services in adult mental health in Hull.

Dan is very passionate about Acceptance and Commitment Therapy and Mentalization-Based Treatment, and uses both approaches in his clinical work. He is also interested in service development with a focus on reflective practice, staff support and helping other professionals develop psychological skills.

He lives in the East Riding of Yorkshire with his wife, who is also a clinical psychologist, and two-year-old daughter.

Chris Brown, MSW, SWE – Mental Health Social Worker

Chris is a social worker from Hull, East Yorkshire. He is passionate about psychosocial models of mental health, and advocacy and social justice for people most marginalised in, and stigmatised by, society.

Chris' initial work began in the local mental health crisis team and acute wards. He also worked at a traditional community mental health setting before joining the Homeless Mental Health Team just over two years ago, where he works with people rough sleeping and precariously housed across the city. It was here that Chris first encountered Pretreatment, and its simplicity and efficacy in connecting with people has transformed his practice. He has delivered training and workshops on Pre-treatment Therapy and other topics across Yorkshire.

Chris is currently training to be a Family Therapist and Systemic Practitioner. After some years away (mainly in Glasgow), Chris returned to East Yorkshire where he now lives with his wife, Becky, and two daughters.

Virginia Bilz, MEd – Special Education

Ginny has worked in the field of special education for over thirty years. She began her career working with juvenile offenders, first, as a teacher and ultimately as principal of a secure treatment facility. After moving into the public school realm, she taught special education at the high school level, teaching students with moderate learning disabilities, emotional disabilities and neurodivergence. Currently retired, she still enjoys working with young people through substitute teaching and participating in summer programs.

Kate Shapiro, BA, JD

Kate lives in Western Massachusetts with her two kids, Hannah and Jonah, and her husband, Dan. She has run and started a number of programs that support individuals living with mental health and substance use disorders that intersect with the courts, housing and other public systems. She is a passionate supporter of the housing-first model and has also dedicated significant time in her career to providing case management services to support individuals in obtaining and maintaining affordable housing. While she and others advocate for national and local housing reform to create more affordable housing for all, Kate also conducts workshops for providers on finding low-income housing in the current complicated system. Kate received the EOHHS statewide Performance Recognition Award in 2021 for her exceptional case management and housing navigation work.

Kate has used her law degree to teach marginalized individuals to advocate for themselves. She is an avid believer in Jay's parallel process model and uses it both in her leadership and direct service work. She continues to search for an agency and role that will allow her to apply her gifts utilizing these Pretreatment values.

Index

Cross-Cultural Dialogues on Homelessness Reveal New Insights

This groundbreaking book presents compelling narratives and innovative approaches for addressing the psychological traumas that can underlie homelessness and is the first to explore in-depth what the US and UK can learn from one another. Authors focus on understanding and applying the precepts of Pretreatment and "Psychologically Informed Environments," as well as effective ways to promote productive dialogue on all levels—with clients, clinicians, advocates, policymakers, researchers, and others. Detailed case studies review and integrate "hands on" practice with Appreciative Inquiry, Open Dialogue, and Common Language Construction methods.

"In *Cross-Cultural Dialogues on Homelessness*, Jay Levy and co-authors provide the conceptual tools, the hitherto 'missing language', needed by practitioners and policymakers working with excluded individuals. This book has been informed by the authors' practice and should come with a warning: it will revolutionise how you work -- irreversibly and, undoubtedly,for the better"

-- Cliona Ni Cheallaigh, MB, MRCP, PhD,
Senior Lecturer in Medical Gerontology, Trinity College (Dublin)

"*Cross Cultural Dialogues on Homelessness* is a timely and important collection of the latest thinking on how we should respond to the traumatic life experiences of so many homeless people. Levy and colleagues suggest a commitment to reflective dialogue will improve both the quality of frontline services and the way policy makers, managers and commissioners think about responding to the needs of people pushed to the margins of our societies."

-- Alex Bax, Chief Executive, (London) Pathway - transforming health services for homeless people

Learn more at www.JaySLevy.com

Jay Levy's *Pretreatment In Action: Interactive Exploration from Homelessness to Housing Stabilization* provides the reader with a wonderfully crafted, detailed step-by-step manual with real-world scenarios on how Pretreatment and the Stages of Engagement play out in the actual work. The vignettes are rich with descriptions that clearly come from a deep repertoire of experience working in the field that gives the reader confidence they are being guided by someone who has been in their shoes. The thoughtful questions and space to reflect add a helpful workbook touch to the feel of the text, and matches the grittiness of the material being covered.

The reader will...

- Understand the 5 principles of a Pretreatment Model through their application to real-life scenarios that depict the world of homelessness, trauma and loss.
- Learn how to utilize Pretreatment Assessment and interventions to promote the engagement process and safety with highly vulnerable people.
- Effectively integrate the stages of Common Language Development with one's own practice of outreach and engagement with under-served persons.
- Experience through interactive exercises and reflecting on case illustrations the importance of facilitating the meaning-making process with both staff and clients.
- Discover an innovative approach to staff supervision based on the integration of Pretreatment principles with Psychologically Informed Environments (PIE) and Open Dialogue approaches to helping

Learn more at www.JaySLevy.com

On any given night, there are over 643,000 homeless people residing in shelters and on the streets across America.

"Levy crafts stories of characters who sear the memory: Old Man Ray, the World War II veteran who resents the VA system and regards himself as the de facto night watchman at Port Authority; Ben who claims to be a prophet disowned in his own country, crucified by the government and enslaved by poverty finds a bridge to the mainstream services and a path to housing through the common language of religious metaphors, including redemption and forgiveness; and others

These stories are deftly interwoven with theory and practice as Levy constructs his developmental model of the engagement and pretreatment process. The outreach worker strives to understand the language and the culture of each homeless individual, builds a bridge to the mainstream services, and helps those providers to understand the special circumstances of these vulnerable people. Levy bears witness to the courage of these pilgrims who wander the streets of our cities, and his poignant book is a testament to the healing power of trusting and enduring relationships."

--Jim O'Connell, MD -- President and Street Physician for Boston Health Care for the Homeless Program

- Experience moving real life stories that demystify homeless outreach and its central objectives and challenges.
- Learn about effective strategies of outreach & engagement with under-served populations.
- Understand and be able to utilize the stages of common language construction in your own practice.
- Learn about pretreatment principles and their applications with persons experiencing untreated major mental illness, addiction, and medical issues.

Learn more at www.JaySLevy.com

This book provides social workers, outreach clinicians, case managers, and concerned community members with a pretreatment guide for assisting homeless couples, youth, and single adults. The interrelationship between Homeless Outreach and Housing First is examined in detail to inform program development and hands on practice. *Pretreatment Guide for Homeless Outreach & Housing First* shares five detailed case studies from the field to elucidate effective ways of helping and to demonstrate how the most vulnerable among us can overcome trauma and homelessness.

Readers will:

- Expand their assessment skills and discover new interventions for helping people who have experienced long-term or chronic homelessness.
- Understand and be able to integrate the stages of common language construction with their own practice.
- Learn about the positive measurable impact of a Housing First approach and its moral, fiscal, and quality of life implications.
- Understand how to better integrate program policy and supervision with Homeless Outreach & Housing First initiatives.
- Learn how to utilize a Pretreatment Approach with couples, youth, and unaccompanied adults experiencing untreated major mental illness and addiction.

"Jay S. Levy's book is essential reading to both people new to the movement to end homelessness and folks who have been in the trenches for many years. Learn how to do effective outreach with the chronic homeless population, and the ins and outs of the Housing First model."

Michael Stoops, Director of Community Organizing National Coalition for the Homeless, Washington, DC

www.ingramcontent.com/pod-product-compliance
Lightning Source LLC
Jackson TN
JSHW011903060625
85476JS00006B/24